D1536545

SILENCIO
Reflective Practices for Nurturing Your Soul

Written by the Leadership Transformations Team

STEPHEN A. MACCHIA, EDITOR

Published by LTI Publications
P.O. Box 338, Lexington, MA 02420
www.leadershiptransformations.org

Cover design: Michelle Blackstone
Interior design: Priya Paulraj
ISBN: 978-0-578-59368-5 (Paperback)

Printed in the United States of America

TABLE OF CONTENTS

INTRODUCTION

The idea for creating monthly spiritual formation resources as a team was first introduced over coffee with Matt Scott, one of our former team members, at our kitchen table. We were looking ahead at how best to resource our wider LTI family with readily accessible resources designed with their souls in mind. We sketched out how best to format them for consistency, brainstormed the first few topics to address, invited teammates to begin writing, and off we went with what became one of our most beloved communication efforts in our 16-year history.

We decided to call each issue "*Silencio*" because the focus of Leadership Transformations' ministry is to help leaders prioritize the care and nurture of their souls. We believe "as the leader goes, so goes the organization…and, more importantly, as the soul of the leader goes, so goes the leader." And we're convinced that slowing life down long enough to listen more attentively to the voice of God is what leads us to become more loving, gracious, and relationally effective as spiritual leaders. Silence (*Silencio* in Latin) is key to that slowing down, in order to listen more intentionally to God and one another, and then to obey God and serve others more faithfully.

Silencio is the first movement of lectio divina (the ancient and timeless process of slowly reading, praying and savoring the sacred text of Scripture) and is a much needed spiritual practice today. Silencing the noises of our external and internal lives is essential to the process of learning how to more purely and sincerely listen. If we are to tend lovingly to the nurturing of our souls, and to help others do likewise, then practicing "*Silencio*" is critical to our effectiveness in life, relationships, and service to others. Our spiritual lives deepen significantly when we are able to be silent before God, listening to the One who has much more important things to say to us than we to him.

This handbook is the net result of over five years of writing, compiling, and distributing *Silencio* one month and topic at a time. The team approach to offering such a practical and helpful spiritual formation resource for the LTI family has been invigorating for all. Nearly two dozen members of our ministry team participated in this effort. Each issue was written from their heart, noticing and reflecting the heart of God, and sharing heart-to-heart with our readers. We've received very positive feedback from our constituency each month and are delighted to now share this monthly, team-created resource in one volume.

The format of *Silencio* is designed for weekly personal reflection and Soul Sabbath use by the reader. There are 52 weekly selections offered herein, with an additional 12 chapters provided for those who wish to add reflection into the Christian Year, via the universally suggested Church Calendar, beginning with the season of Advent, and continuing through Ordinary Time.

Contents provided per chapter include:

1. an overview of the topic written by a member of the LTI team;
2. an historically timeless public domain hymn for prayerful reflection;
3. questions for additional reflection;
4. spiritual practices for personal application; and
5. a prayer of illumination as you culminate your reflections.

In addition, in the back of the book we offer an Appendix of additional suggested spiritual formation resources for your consideration and exploration per topic covered in each chapter of the book.

As you utilize this spiritual formation resource, you might want to invite a friend or small group of associates or spiritual companions to join you. We have found it deeply meaningful to share in common a resource like *Silencio* among spiritual friends, either close in proximity or with others you know in other parts of the country or world. Meeting periodically for shared reflection helps to solidify your experience and deepen your friendship with God and others in your relational orbit. We can also attest to the fact that sharing such disciplines among your own ministry team will significantly shape the spiritual health of your community of servant-leaders. The Kingdom is advanced in ways that are much more readily apparent to those who pray together in this way. Try it and let us know how it goes.

Special thanks to all those who contributed to this workbook. The following 22 names are members of the LTI team, both past and present, who wrote and compiled their particular chapter(s) which are noted and included herein. I am personally indebted to each of them for their faithful friendship, partnership in ministry, and their sacrificial service in all of our behalf.

Kevin Antlitz
Rick Anderson
Meah Hearington Arakaki
Diana Curren Bennett
Adele Ahlberg Calhoun
Susan Porterfield Currie
John French
Tom Griffith
Gayle Heaslip
Stephen Macchia
Joellen Maurer
Genalin Niere-Metcalf
Sage Paik
Warren Schuh
Matt Scott
Suz Skinner
Jeremy Stefano
Patricia Trewern
Br. David Vryhof, SSJE
Angela Wisdom
David Wu
Ted Wueste

Finally, it's important to note that all members of the LTI team have contributed their time and effort to this project with the joyful acknowledgement that all sales proceeds will directly benefit the ministry of Leadership Transformations. Through your purchase of this spiritual formation resource, we thank you for your support of our mission and ministry. And we pray God uses this material in powerful, life-changing, soul-nurturing ways. The ripple effects will be seen in the transformed hearts and lives of those we serve on a daily basis.

Prayerfully and gratefully for the Leadership Transformations Team,

Stephen A. Macchia
Founder and President, Leadership Transformations, Inc.
Editor, *Silencio: Reflective Practices for Nurturing Your Soul*
www.LeadershipTransformations.org

PRACTICES

1. LECTIO DIVINA

JOHN FRENCH

◆

"It's amazing how the Scriptures came alive!" exclaimed a spiritual friend, after following the suggestion to try reading the Scriptures slowly and out loud in his prayer closet. He had read the Bible all his life; sometimes the text was full of life and challenge. Recently, however, his devotional life was more mechanical, simply going through the motions. Here was a serious Christian going through a dry spell. Deciding to read through the Bible in a year, at breakneck speed, he completed his assignment . . . but he sensed very little of the voice of God in his life.

Reading the Bible aloud, meditatively and slowly, aids one's hearing God in prayer. Is this some newfangled reading of Scripture from the latest author? No, it is a style that is as old as the Bible. St Benedict of Nursa, a 6th-century organizer of monks who aided students in their study of Scripture, is often credited with the organizing structure of sacred reading known as Lectio Divina.

Lectio Divina (meaning sacred or devotional reading) is not Bible study. It is more accurately likened to the praying of Scripture. It is prayerfully reading the biblical text more with the heart than as an exercise of the intellect. Lectio Divina does not replace Bible study. It complements and enhances it so as to let God address our hearts as well as our minds, thus leading the reader to deeper transformation. Too often we read Scripture as a devotional duty rather than an appointment with the living God. When we slow down and listen, it allows us the opportunity to ruminate over a love letter as opposed to reading and analyzing a bill from a vendor.

This fourfold way to practice sacred reading is offered (with an assist from Richard Peace):

1. Lectio (reading with a listening spirit): Read the Scripture slowly. Watch for a key phrase or word that jumps out at you or promises to have special meaning for you. It is better to dwell profoundly on one word or phrase than to skim the surface of several chapters. Read with your own life and choices in mind.

2. Meditatio (reflecting on what we are "hearing"): Reflect on a word or phrase. Let the special word or phrase that you discovered in the first reading sink into your heart. Bring mind, will, and emotions to the task. Be like Mary, Jesus' mother, who heard the angel's announcement and "treasured" and "pondered" what she had heard (Luke 2:19).

3. Oratio (praying in response to this hearing): Respond to what you have read. Form a prayer that expresses your response to the idea, then "pray it back to God." What you have read is woven through what you tell God.

4. Contemplatio (contemplating what we will carry forward into our lives): Rest in God's Word. Let the text soak into your deepest being, savoring an encounter with God and truth. When ready, move toward the moment in which you ask God to show you how to live out what you have experienced.

The ancient practice of Lectio also includes Silencio (beginning with silence) and Incarnatio (ending with the living out of the Word in one's daily life). Don't feel rigidly tied to this structure. Allow your heart to connect with God. As a result, may God bless the reading and receiving of his Word.

"Let the message of Christ dwell among you richly as you
teach and admonish one another with all wisdom through psalms,
hymns, and songs from the Spirit, singing to God with gratitude in your hearts."
—Colossians 3:16

BREAK THOU THE BREAD OF LIFE
A HYMN BY MARY A. LATHBURY, 1877

Break Thou the Bread of Life, Dear Lord, to me,
As Thou didst break the loaves beside the sea;
Beyond the sacred page I seek Thee, Lord;
My spirit pants for Thee, O Living Word.

Thou art the Bread of Life, O Lord, to me,
Thy holy Word, the Truth that saveth me;
Give me to eat and live, with Thee above;
Teach me to love Thy truth, For Thou art Love.

Bless Thou the truth, dear Lord, to me, to me,
As Thou didst bless the bread by Galilee;
Then shall all bondage cease, all fetters fall;
And I shall find my peace, my all in all.

Oh, send Thy Spirit, Lord, Now unto me,
That He may touch my eyes, And make me see;
Show me the truth concealed, Within Thy Word,
And in Thy Book revealed, I see the Lord.

REFLECTION QUESTIONS

As you reflect upon your past study and reading of Scripture, how has God spoken to you?

What new ways might the Spirit be stirring in your heart through the practice of lectio?

Would you characterize yourself as someone who reads through the Scriptures very quickly? If so, would you receive this invitation to slow down and deeply engage with the Word of God?

As you prayerfully sit with the Scriptures, are you able to meditate on a specific word or phrase throughout the day? the week ahead? an even longer period of time?

SPIRITUAL PRACTICES

In your prayer closet, try following the ancient rhythms of Lectio Divina as you prayerfully read the Bible. Begin your time with silence and prepare your heart to receive the Word.

Read/listen: Read aloud a short passage of Scripture. As you read, listen for the word or phrase that speaks to you. What is the Spirit drawing attention to?

Meditate: Repeat aloud the word or phrase to which you are drawn. Make connections between it and your life. What is God saying to you by means of this word or phrase?

Pray: Now take these thoughts and offer them back to God in prayer, giving thanks, asking for guidance, asking for forgiveness, and resting in God's love. What is God leading you to pray?

Contemplate: Move from the activity of prayer to the stillness of contemplation. Simply rest in God's presence. Stay open to God. Listen to God. Remain in peace and silence before God. How is God revealing himself to you? (Based on Richard Peace's *Contemplative Bible Reading*)

As you conclude your time in the Word, invite God to empower you to incarnate his Word in your daily life, even in the day ahead.

A Prayer of Illumination:
Shine within our hearts, Glorious One, the pure light of your divine knowledge. And illumine our minds and hearts that we may understand and embrace the treasures of your Holy Word. Amen.

2. LISTENING PRAYER

SUSAN PORTERFIELD CURRIE

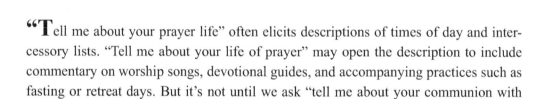

"Tell me about your prayer life" often elicits descriptions of times of day and intercessory lists. "Tell me about your life of prayer" may open the description to include commentary on worship songs, devotional guides, and accompanying practices such as fasting or retreat days. But it's not until we ask "tell me about your communion with God" that we start to get at the heart of prayer.

That's because prayer is a face-to-face, heart-to-heart, mind-to-mind, soul-to-soul relating between God and us, through his Holy Spirit in us. Like any good conversation between two people who love and respect each other, it is not a series of monologues flung out in hopes that the other is paying attention—us, talking at God with our lists of praises and intercessions, God talking at us in long passages of Scripture. It is thoughtfully attentive and responsive, weaving back and forth, each to the other. While Scripture, God's revelation in creation, and our experiences and concerns of the day may all enter into the conversation, it's the back-and-forth around this content that makes the conversation prayer.

Listening Prayer begins by stilling all competing noise. Once you're mature in Listening Prayer, you may find that you intuitively hear the voice of the Holy Spirit even in the midst of other conversations. But in general, a diffused attention makes it hard for anyone to listen well. So still the sounds around you—sounds of media, of machines, of others' voices. And try to still the sounds within you—your own words, your own busy thoughts, your own analysis of the text before you. Still these sounds, and say, with young Samuel, "Speak, Lord, for your servant is listening." (1 Samuel 1:9)

And then notice what you notice. Sometimes, on occasion, you may hear a voice, but more often you'll notice impressions—thoughts appear in your mind, a feeling whispers past your heart, a sense glistens at the edge of your awareness. Hold what you notice before God, asking "Is this from you?" and let the conversation develop. Anytime you find yourself taking the conversational ball and running with it, slow down, return to silence, and pray again, "Speak, Lord…" What you're trying to listen to is God's Spirit, praying inside you with groans too deep for words (Romans 8:26-27).

Discernment—learning the voice of the Holy Spirit—comes over time, with familiarity. But it's helpful to ask a few discernment questions of what you have been noticing: Is this in line with what God speaks in Scripture? Is it in line with what I know of God? If this is of the Spirit, does it reveal the fruit of the Spirit? Am I willing to bring this before trusted spiritual friends and seek their discernment? Am I willing to wait? If something is of the Holy Spirit, it will last; if not, it will be revealed as false or it will fall away.

God, who loves you and calls you into communion as his Beloved, is very near. Be still, and listen.

"The Spirit helps us in our weakness. We do not know what we ought to pray for, but the Spirit himself intercedes for us through wordless groans. And he who searches our hearts knows the mind of the Spirit, because the Spirit intercedes for God's people in accordance with the will of God."
—Romans 8:26-27

"We learn to listen in prayer. Then, in time, the whole of our lives will be marked by our capacity to listen."
—Gordon Smith, The Voice of Jesus: Discernment, Prayer and the Witness of the Spirit

COME DOWN, O LOVE DIVINE
A HYMN BY BIANCO DA SIENA (d. 1434), trans.
RICHARD FREDRICK LITTLEDALE, 1867

Come down, O Love divine, Seek out this soul of mine
And visit it with Your own ardor glowing;
O Comforter, draw near, Within my heart appear,
And kindle it, Your holy flame bestowing.

O let it freely burn, Till earthly passions turn
To dust and ashes in its heat consuming;
And let Your glorious light Shine ever on my sight,
And clothe me round, the while my path illuming.

And so the yearning strong, With which the soul will long
Shall far outpass the power of human telling;
For none can guess God's grace, Till Love creates a place
Wherein the Holy Spirit makes a dwelling.

REFLECTION QUESTIONS

What makes for a good conversation between you and another person? What would it look like for this to characterize your prayer?

When you're listening attentively to another, how do you pay attention with your body? With your ears, your eyes, your other senses? What would it look like for this to characterize your prayer?

Think of a time when you've been sure you have heard the Lord. What made you sure?

How do you notice the Holy Spirit inside you? How do others you respect in the spiritual life notice the work of God's Spirit? Have a spiritual conversation about this on a frequent basis.

SPIRITUAL PRACTICES

Train your senses to be more attentive by sitting outside in a quiet place, and notice what you notice with your eyes. Then close your eyes and notice with your ears. Notice with your scent, with your skin…perhaps you might want to journal your noticings.

Take five minutes to try Listening Prayer. Settle in; begin with the prayer "Speak, Lord, I am listening." After something—anything—comes to your senses, ask the Lord, "Is this you, Holy Spirit?" Listen.

Jot down in your journal the things that seem to have any significance in your listening. At the end of the week, note any themes or recurring awarenesses.

Discuss your experience with a spiritual friend or guide. Discern together whether and how you have been hearing God's voice of love as you listened to him in prayer.

A Prayer of Illumination:
I keep asking that the God of our Lord Jesus Christ, the glorious Father, may give you the Spirit of wisdom and revelation, so that you may know him better. I pray that the eyes of your heart may be enlightened… (Ephesians 1:17-18).

3. REFLECTION: REMEMBER AND GIVE THANKS

STEPHEN A. MACCHIA

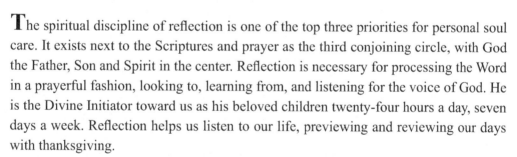

The spiritual discipline of reflection is one of the top three priorities for personal soul care. It exists next to the Scriptures and prayer as the third conjoining circle, with God the Father, Son and Spirit in the center. Reflection is necessary for processing the Word in a prayerful fashion, looking to, learning from, and listening for the voice of God. He is the Divine Initiator toward us as his beloved children twenty-four hours a day, seven days a week. Reflection helps us listen to our life, previewing and reviewing our days with thanksgiving.

However, if we are not practicing any of the myriad options for the discipline of reflection, we miss so much of what the Lord has in store for us to receive from his generous and loving hand. The more we attend to the practice of reflection, the more we ultimately learn, discover, and receive from God. As one mystic of old mused, "Action without reflection is meaningless action" (source unknown). Therefore, without reflection our life may be full, but not very fulfilling.

There are countless ways to practice reflective disciplines: journaling, photography, creative arts, holy conversations, pausing, noticing, attending, wondering, pondering. We can reflect alone and in the quietness of solitude, and we can reflect with a loved one in the daily-ness of our relational connections. We can sit with a single verse or segment of the biblical text, holding that verse(s) prayerfully or interviewing the text in an exploratory fashion.

The key to unlocking this spiritual practice is recognizing why we do so. The singularly most important reason is that we are generally a forgetful people. We need help remembering, and in turn, giving thanks. If we believe that God is indeed initiating toward us 24x7, then it's incumbent upon us to pay attention, notice, recall, and give thanks. The people of God have been a forgetful bunch for millennia, and there are many times God calls his children to remember…even if it means placing a pile of rocks on the other side of the sea to remember and give thanks for God's faithful leading and protection. (Read Joshua 4 to recall the Rocks of Remembrance after the children of God safely crossed the Jordan River.)

The pinnacle call to remembrance comes when Jesus institutes the Lord's Supper as a reflective practice for the ultimate Eucharisteo for remembering regularly the sacrificial death of Jesus for our sins on the Cross. The life, death, and resurrection of Jesus are wrapped up in this incredible time of remembrance known as the sacrament or ordinance of Communion. We remember and we give thanks, over and over again, in similar fashion each time. Why? So that we will never ever forget.

To choose the discipline of reflection is to choose the practice of recollection, recalibrating our souls by remembering the gifts God gives us in this life (the good, the hard, the challenging, and the beautiful) . . . and always with a grateful heart.

"These stones are to be a memorial to the people of Israel forever."
—Joshua 4:7

"God is reaching out to me, speaking to me, and it is up to me
to learn to be polite enough to pay attention."
—Virginia R. Mollenkott

NOW THANK WE ALL OUR GOD
A HYMN BY MARTIN RINKART, 1636

Now thank we all our God, with heart and hands and voices,
Who wondrous things has done, in Whom this world rejoices;
Who from our mothers' arms has blessed us on our way
With countless gifts of love, and still is ours today.

O may this bounteous God through all our life be near us,
With ever joyful hearts and blessèd peace to cheer us;
And keep us in His grace, and guide us when perplexed;
And free us from all ills, in this world and the next!

All praise and thanks to God the Father now be given;
The Son and Him Who reigns with Them in highest Heaven;
The one eternal God, whom earth and Heaven adore;
For thus it was, is now, and shall be evermore.

REFLECTION QUESTIONS

In what way do you feel invited by God to foster or enhance one or more spiritual practices of reflection?

With whom can you journey together into a deeper commitment to practice reflective disciplines? How will you encourage one another?

For what or whom are you led to recall with thanksgiving? How will you share such a recollection with another spiritual friend today?

How can you approach the Lord's Supper differently, the next time you are gathered with your faith community, to more intentionally and reflectively remember and give thanks?

SPIRITUAL PRACTICES

Consider adding more reflective practices into your times of silence, solitude, and prayer. Might God perhaps be inviting you to renew your spiritual journal or the practice of Examen?

What do you currently collect that reminds you of experiences, relationships, or memories you don't want to forget (i.e., crosses, rocks, etc.)? Is it time to catalog or organize them?

What could you do to practice the discipline of reflection in a brand new way, i.e., drawing a picture, contemplating creation, or writing a prayer?

Write out questions you'd like to ask yourself regularly to enhance your spiritual discipline of reflection.

A Prayer of Illumination:
Lord, I long to rediscover the freshness of my relationship with you and recommit myself to practicing the daily disciplines of prayer, Scripture reading, and reflection. May this kind of discipline-ship mark my life in the depths of my inner being, and may the choices I make each new day bring me back in step with your heart for my life. In the precious name of my dear Savior, Jesus. Amen.

4. JOURNALING

DIANA CURREN BENNETT

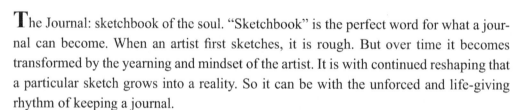

The Journal: sketchbook of the soul. "Sketchbook" is the perfect word for what a journal can become. When an artist first sketches, it is rough. But over time it becomes transformed by the yearning and mindset of the artist. It is with continued reshaping that a particular sketch grows into a reality. So it can be with the unforced and life-giving rhythm of keeping a journal.

As a teenager, you may have kept your "Five-Year Diary" well hidden and full of chronological events as well as hopes, disappointments, and gossip. Keeping a diary can become a serious chore, even if it's eventually discarded. While being challenged by the discipline of journaling in later years, one may look back to that tedious job of keeping a daily diary. However, with time, creativity, and a better understanding of what a journal could be, interest can be renewed.

The journal is like a spiritual diary. The flip side of the dreaded diary, the journal is not a chronology of "what I did today," but a personal reflective response concerning various aspects of the spiritual life. The journal is a place to reflect on our state of soul, our various moods and their implications, our personal disciplines or lack thereof, our failures, celebrations, concerns, sins, prayers, and yearnings. Anything that might be involved in the development of knowing God in a deeper relationship and knowing ourselves through the lens of God's love and grace can be included. Listening attentively to the voice of Jesus and recording what we hear are amazing moments of illumination, the thrill of discovery. Discovery becomes a loving gift from God often erased by time and memory. Writing it down helps us to remember, rereading entries increases our trust, and seeing answered prayer gives us hope and a segue into deeper worship and thanksgiving.

Journaling is not for everyone. It is not commanded in Scripture as a practice for us. It was however, commanded to Moses by God in Exodus 17:14. Most of the time we want to keep our journal private. And it should be. There are times when people share portions of their journal to encourage others and to glorify God with his presence and works, but generally the journal should be private. When we know that the journal is between God and us, we can be honest with reflections, anger, forgiveness, joys, sorrows, frustrations, and yearnings. As one seminary professor liked to quip, "Now I lay me down to sleep, I pray the Lord my soul to keep. If I should die before I wake, throw my journal in the lake!"

The journal gives us insight into our own growth. It helps us clarify our priorities and assists us in problem solving. It stimulates accountability and authenticity. It springs from creativity and allows the poorest of artists to sketch visions and yearnings. Ultimately, the journal can become an integral part of God's image for us to be developed as he re-forms our longings and goals into his handiwork in our soul transformation. May God give you insight as to whether this is a rhythm he is inviting you to explore. If so, may your journal bring you great joy.

"Then the Lord said to Moses, 'Write this on a scroll as something to be remembered and make sure that Joshua hears it, because I will completely blot out the memory of Amalek from under the heaven.'"
—Exodus 17:14

"A journal is more than a diary; it does not so much record our days as record our spirits...our inner world is so murky, so hidden, yet so potent. To know oneself from within is so powerful, so difficult, so vital."
—Dr. Richard Peace, Spiritual Journaling and the Witness of the Spirit

HOW FIRM A FOUNDATION
A HYMN ATTRIBUTED VARIOUSLY TO JOHN KEENE, KIRKHAM AND JOHN KEITH, 1787

How firm a foundation, ye saints of the Lord,
Is laid for your faith in His excellent Word!
What more can He say than to you He hath said,
To you, who for refuge to Jesus have fled?

Fear not, I am with thee, O be not dismayed,
For I am thy God, I will still give thee aid;
I'll strengthen thee, help thee, and cause thee to stand,
Upheld by my gracious, omnipotent hand.

When thru the deep waters I call thee to go,
The rivers of woe shall not thee overflow;
For I will be with thee thy troubles to bless,
And sanctify to thee thy deepest distress.

The soul that on Jesus hath leaned for repose,
I will not, I will not desert to his foes.
That soul, tho all hell should endeavor to shake,
I'll never, no, never, no, never forsake!

REFLECTION QUESTIONS

Although journals are helpful for past and future, journals also become vital tools for us to live in the present with God. In what way might recording prayers, concerns, questions, or celebrations help you with greater clarity to see your life, feel your life, and live your life with God?

What would a journal entry look like for you if you were discerning an important decision?

If you begin a journal by writing your "life with God" story, what events and insights might you experience through your written word as it is laced with God's written Word? Are you willing to share journal entries with others? If so, with whom and under what condition? Why would keeping your journal private be important for you?

SPIRITUAL PRACTICES

Decide, through prayer, what God might be inviting you to do in beginning a journal. Perhaps for you it will be seasons of the year, weekly reflections, Bible study, or situational moments. There's no right or wrong way to journal.

Find a book suitable to use as a journal. Begin by asking the Holy Spirit to guide you as you write your thoughts. Record the date, and write down what comes to mind. It might be a prayer, an insight from your Bible reading, or a nagging situation that needs to be expressed on paper.

Consider beginning your journal with sketching out your personal spiritual vision. Remember, drawings are fun and instructive and not graded!

Try using colored pencils or markers in your journal. Watch how the multiple colors help to highlight and illuminate various aspects of your personal and spiritual life.

A Prayer of Illumination:
Lord, as you spoke each of your children into being, you know us completely through your gracious love. Encourage us to journal if that is one venue of insight for seeing ourselves through the lens of your redemption. Holy Spirit, guide our hand and thoughts as we reflect on our life lived in the power of your transforming love. In Jesus' name we pray. Amen.

5. EXAMEN

SAGE PAIK

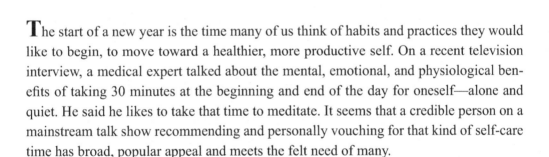

The start of a new year is the time many of us think of habits and practices they would like to begin, to move toward a healthier, more productive self. On a recent television interview, a medical expert talked about the mental, emotional, and physiological benefits of taking 30 minutes at the beginning and end of the day for oneself—alone and quiet. He said he likes to take that time to meditate. It seems that a credible person on a mainstream talk show recommending and personally vouching for that kind of self-care time has broad, popular appeal and meets the felt need of many.

The truth is that we live harried, anxiety-filled, on-the-go, technology-driven lives. That fast pace may begin early in life when parents overschedule their children. It continues into adulthood as people feel the need to remain busy in order to feel important. Twenty-four hours seem a few hours too short of what would be nice to have in a day: things around the house are never "done," and the stream of emails and demands for our time seem unending. Too easily we wrap our sense of worth and pride around the frenzy of life instead of in the costly, steady, spacious love and grace for us of God in Christ. Still, something deep within longs for slower, longer, fuller breaths. And rest.

Our ancient Christian heritage calls to us with such an invitation. The Ignatians have given us the long-practiced way of solitary, quiet reflection called the daily Examen.

Through it, we take time to deliberately notice God and discern His leading in the internal thoughts and external events of our everyday life. This practice instructs us to become aware of God's presence, review the day with gratitude, pay attention to our emotions, choose one feature of the day and pray from it while we look toward tomorrow.

Our common longing and need to pause and care for ourselves, our need to notice the presence and leading of God... could in fact be the Spirit-formed product of daily examen, which is a form of worship. Worship—not of the church community, Sunday morning sort, but the kind that is done alone at the end of a full day. Worship that is putting down things that are not quite done. Worship that trusts in Him that it's okay. Worship that is washing up and sitting or lying down in bed giving our tired bodies and minds to His care again. Worship that acknowledges His goodness and love. Humble-grateful-adoring. The One who loved us while we were yet His enemies. The safety of opening all of our heart for the searching, exposing, advocating work of the Holy Spirit in us. Seeing and listening as He lovingly reminds us of moments in our day and reveals ways of repentance, obedience, and gratitude. Receiving His mercy and satisfied grace. Anticipating a more-right relationship with Him and our neighbor. And even if we fall asleep mid-examen, He is still able to lead us into our knowing and obeying Him. His grace is sufficient for us. It is well with our soul.

"Search me, God, and know my heart; test me and know my anxious thoughts. See if there is any offensive way in me, and lead me in the way everlasting."
—Psalm 139:23-24

"My flesh and my heart may fail, but God is the strength of my heart and my portion forever."
—Psalm 73:26

BE THOU MY VISION
A HYMN BY DALLAN FORGAIL, 6TH CENTURY

Be Thou my Vision, O Lord of my heart;
Naught be all else to me, save that Thou art.
Thou my best Thought, by day or by night,
Waking or sleeping, Thy presence my light.

Be Thou my Wisdom, and Thou my true Word;
I ever with Thee and Thou with me, Lord;
Thou my great Father, I Thy true son;
Thou in me dwelling, and I with Thee one.

Riches I heed not, nor man's empty praise,
Thou mine Inheritance, now and always
Thou and Thou only, first in my heart,
High King of Heaven, my Treasure Thou art.

High King of Heaven, my victory won,
May I reach Heaven's joys, O bright Heaven's Sun!
Heart of my own heart, whatever befall,
Still be my Vision, O Ruler of all.

REFLECTION QUESTIONS

Looking back on the day's events, which have been most life-giving? Which have been most life-draining?

What are the things that led you toward God today? What are the things that led you away from God?

When did you have the greatest sense of leaning into your true self (an identity that is firmly rooted in the love of Christ)?

When did you have a sense of leaning into your false self (ways in which we strive to find our identity apart from Christ)?

As you sit prayerfully and listen to the stirrings of the Spirit, what is God's invitation to you as you pay attention to the day's events?

SPIRITUAL PRACTICES

Consider ending your day with holy Examen. Become aware of God's presence. Ask the Holy Spirit to increase your awareness of God's promised presence.

Review the day with gratitude. Give thanks and celebrate the gifts that you received from God and others.

Pay attention to your emotions. List a few feelings that were present throughout the day (i.e., embarrassment, fear, elation, contentment).

Choose one feature of the day and pray from it. Ask the Holy Spirit to bring one element of your day to mind. Focus specifically on that experience. Sit with it prayerfully.

Look toward tomorrow. As you look, allow God to shape a prayer within you.

A Prayer of Illumination:

As I lay me down to sleep, my soul asks of God, show me what you want me to see. Was there any person I may have hurt or been ungracious or ungentle toward today? Reveal the motives of my heart. Was I selfish? Was I cowardly? Was I proud? Remind me what I forgot to thank you for today. Thank you. Give me the grace to go check to see if I offended someone, to be vulnerable, to make peace, to be more quick to notice you. Make me more of who you have already made me in Christ. For the service of others and to your glory and delight. Amen.

6. CONFESSION

DAVID WU

Confession. The word alone evokes a wide range of emotions within each of us. For some, it may evoke childhood memories of being forced to "fess up" after getting caught in an act of disobedience. For others, it may bring a great sense of peace and relief to finally disclose a hidden secret. Either way, at its core, confession is very simply an admission of guilt. And we generally don't enjoy talking about our own sin, thus avoiding conversations that may surface our feelings of guilt or shame.

Confession can be scary because it's an admission of something negative about ourselves, be it something we've done or some fault in our character. And the less we've developed a relationship with someone, the more fearful we become of true confession. Why? Because we do not know how the other person is going to respond. Perhaps their opinion of us will change. Or maybe our confession might lead them to reject us. But in the context of an intimate relationship that is characterized by forgiveness, grace, and love, confession can actually become very liberating. In fact, a rhythm of confession and forgiveness is necessary for a thriving relationship. The healthiest marriages are characterized by honesty, providing a place where admission of faults and confession of wrongdoings are safely exchanged. Friendships thrive when they foster a safe place to admit that we've been wronged or have wronged another. And though it might feel counter-intuitive, the safest place of confession resides in our relationship with God.

Moment by moment, God is graciously seeking a restored relationship with us. Still, many of us go about our lives bound up, fearful of fully disclosing our sin and "coming clean." If this is the case, it is likely that our perception of God is such that we feel threatened or unsafe. When we view God as a wrathful, angry God who needs to be appeased by our confession, we are unable to see confession as a loving initiative toward intimacy. Feelings of guilt, shame, and fear overwhelm us. But we can change our minds! Rather than threatening us, confession can become an invitation to receive a renewed fellowship and communion with God. Because his love is unfailing and he is a gracious, forgiving God, confession comes to us as a gift disguised.

In the Scriptures, we see the example of the Church of Laodicea in Revelation 3. There is no doubt the sin of lukewarmness is distasteful to our Lord. And yet, his posture toward us in verse 20 is this: he stands at the door and knocks, waiting for us to come to him. The act of confession is like opening the door to our Savior who is knocking and waiting. Christ remains eager to invite us into restored fellowship with him. So for those who have walked some time with Jesus, they no longer expect Christ to recoil or reject them because of their faults, flaws, and sins. They understand that their Savior loves them with an everlasting love. They've experienced how eager Jesus is to forgive and to restore. They recognize that no matter how distasteful their sin may be, their Lord is even more eager for them to experience restored fellowship and communion.

"I acknowledged my sin to you, and I did not cover my iniquity; I said, "I will confess my transgressions to the LORD," and you forgave the iniquity of my sin. Selah."
—Psalm 32:5 ESV

"To confess your sins to God is not to tell [God] anything [God] doesn't already know. Until you confess them, however, they are the abyss between you. When you confess them, they become the bridge." —
—Frederick Buechner, Beyond Words

IT IS WELL WITH MY SOUL
A HYMN BY HORATIO G. SPAFFORD, 1873

When peace, like a river,
attendeth my way,
When sorrows like sea billows roll;
Whatever my lot, Thou hast taught me to say,
It is well, it is well with my soul.
Refrain: It is well with my soul, It is well,
it is well with my soul.

Though Satan should buffet,
though trials should come,
Let this blest assurance control,
That Christ has regarded my helpless estate,
And hath shed His own blood for my soul.
Refrain

My sin, oh, the bliss
of this glorious thought!
My sin, not in part but the whole,
Is nailed to the cross, and I bear it no more,
Praise the Lord, praise the Lord, O my soul!
Refrain

And Lord, haste the day
when my faith shall be sight,
The clouds be rolled back as a scroll;
The trump shall resound,
and the Lord shall descend,
Even so, it is well with my soul.
Refrain

REFLECTION QUESTIONS

What sins have I committed (against God, self, or others) this day? Freely confess those to the Lord and, if appropriate, to another.

How does your view of God's love for you affect your ability to fully confess your sin? Are you carrying an undue burden of guilt or shame because of a particular sin you've committed? Are you willing to open-handedly release that burden to God?

Do you view confession as a burdensome obligation or an invitation? Why?

Confess your joy and delight in the Lord. How does your giving voice to the confession of loving faithfulness affect your countenance in Christ?

SPIRITUAL PRACTICES

Use this prayer as a guide to confession: *Gracious God, my sins are too heavy to carry, too real to hide, and too deep to undo. Forgive me of what my lips tremble to name and what my heart can no longer bear. I confess my _____ and I humbly ask for your forgiveness.*

Pray this prayer, as an Assurance of Pardon: *Almighty God, who does freely pardon all who repent and turn to Him, now fulfill in every contrite heart the promise of redeeming grace; forgiving all our sins, and cleansing us from an evil conscience; through the perfect sacrifice of Christ Jesus our Lord. Amen.*

Share your confession with a trusted friend (James 5:16).

Add confession into your daily spiritual routines, and invite others in your circle of influence to consider the freedom and forgiveness that result from a heart of confession.

A Prayer of Illumination:
Merciful Lord, we confess that with us there is an abundance of sin, but in you there is the fullness of righteousness and abundance of mercy. We are spiritually poor, but you are rich and in Jesus Christ came to be merciful to the poor. Strengthen our faith and trust in you. We are empty vessels that need to be filled; fill us. We are weak in faith; strengthen us. We are cold in love; warm us, and make our hearts fervent for you that our love may go out to one another and to our neighbors. We pray these things in faith, through Jesus Christ our Lord. Amen.

7. FASTING

DIANA CURREN BENNETT

$\diamond$

Fasting is an ancient practice. In Jewish tradition, fasting had two primary purposes. First, it expressed personal or national repentance for sin. And second, fasting prepared oneself inwardly for receiving the inner strength and grace to complete a mission of faithful service in God's name. Over the years this spiritual discipline has become more than the original biblical combination of "prayer and fasting." At the core, however, remains the same intention--a healthy discipline rooted in freedom that brings our soul into deeper communion with God.

Fasting creates the venue for stepping away from our culture and false idols and into the presence of God. With a posture of open hands, we release self-directed desires, distractions, and actions that dominate our lives. Fasting is also rooted in God's invitation to us. Thus, we do not approach it for personal attention or from the pressures of peers. It is safe to say today's fasting practices include abstaining not only from food (as shown in the biblical examples) but also from news, media, shopping, entertainment, information systems, and other aspects of life.

With fasting, we humbly yearn for God's powerful presence. We mourn over our lack of time in seeking his face; we weep as we confess our sins. Often, we are flooded with grief over life's circumstances. And along with prayer, we fast from food as one crying out to God for healing, salvation, and forgiveness. In the act of release and obedience, we fast to curtail actions and addictions that take our focus away from God's centrality in our daily lives. We fast in preparation for Christ's coming again and call out to him to come quickly. We fast over our spiritual weakness.

"Even now," declares the Lord, "return to me with all your heart with fasting and weeping and mourning." Joel 2:12

Fasting provides opportunities for us to back away from excess (perhaps frivolous delights) to allow God to form healthier pathways in our unforced rhythms of grace. Most often, fasting is a voluntary denial of something for a specific time and purpose by individuals or communities. It becomes a practice of embracing God's presence and a desire to deeply commune with him. It must not be for self-punishment. Instead, it provides space and time through prayer to enable us to joyfully listen to God's voice. In this, we enter into his sufferings and are enlivened by his Spirit. Yes, we call out to his Spirit to descend upon our hearts and fill us with his love and presence.

When God invites us by our inner yearnings and desires to practice the discipline of fasting, it becomes an agreement or commitment between God and us. We are warned that prideful boasting about what we are fasting from is not received as an offering to our Lord. Thus, our fasting must not center on the way we appear to others or what they think of us. Our fasting is unto the Lord.

Seek the Lord. Ask him for suggestions. Listen to his voice. Fasting is not so much about what you give up as about what replaces that time and attention. And in hungering for God, yearning to hear his voice, and crying out in prayer, we begin to notice his marvelous invitations to us. May it be so for you.

"Fasting confirms our utter dependence upon God by finding in him a source of sustenance beyond food. Through it, we learn by experience that God's word to us is a life substance, that it is not food ('bread') alone that gives life, but also the words that proceed from the mouth of God (Matthew 4:4). We learn that we too have meat to eat that the world does not know about (John 4:32, 34). Fasting unto our Lord is therefore feasting—feasting on him and on doing his will."
— Dallas Willard, The Spirit of the Disciplines

"Fasting helps us keep our balance in life. How easily we begin to allow nonessentials to take precedence in our lives. How quickly we crave things we do not need until we are enslaved by them. Fasting helps us realign our cravings, brings us freedom, and positions us to experience the fullness of Christ."
— Richard Foster, Celebration of Discipline.

SPIRIT OF GOD, DESCEND UPON MY HEART
A HYMN BY GEORGE CROLY, 1854

Spirit of God, descend upon my heart;
Wean it from earth, thro' all its pulses move.
Stoop to my weakness, mighty as thou art;
And make me love Thee as I ought to love.

Hast Thou not bid us love Thee, God and King?
All, all Thine own-- soul, heart and strength and mind.
I see Thy cross; there teach my heart to cling;
O let me seek Thee, and O let me find.

Teach me to feel that Thou art always nigh;
Teach me the struggles of the soul to bear.
To check the rising doubt, the rebel sigh;
Teach me the patience of unanswered prayer.

Teach me to love Thee as Thine angels love;
One holy passion filling all my frame.
The baptism of the heav'n-descended Dove;
My heart an altar and Thy love the flame.

REFLECTION QUESTIONS

What are some of the barriers for you in beginning a discipline of fasting?

If you have never fasted, what might the invitation from God be to you? Is there something in your life that is spinning out of control or taking control? Is there a yearning to go deeper in your relationship with God? If so, ask what this fast would look like.

If the purpose of fasting is to make space for extended prayer, what might you fast from to create that time and space?

How does God tend to communicate with you? His Word? Inner nudging? Community?

In what way would a prayer partner or spiritual director assist you in future fasting?

Why is it important to keep a fast confidential, just between you and God?

SPIRITUAL PRACTICES

In your silence and solitude, ask God if he is inviting you into a discipline of fasting.

If you sense an invitation from God, inquire what this fasting would look like. Remember this is private between you and God and perhaps shared with a soul friend.

If you are yearning for a deeper experience of God, be intentional about following through with what you have heard God bring to your attention.

If you practice prayer and fasting, consider why, how, and for what time period this practice can be implemented.

One of the best ways to choose what to fast from is to notice what matters most to you and what keeps you from living with a healthy dependence upon God. Noticing our "attachments" helps us to consciously release them and prayerfully detach from them as we fast.

A Prayer of Illumination:
O Lord, my God, my soul thirsts for you. I yearn to hear your voice and to experience deep communion with you. My desire is to know you and your path for my life. Please show me practices and habits that I can cease for a season in order to pray more often and be transformed by your powerful Holy Spirit. Amen.

8. HOLY EATING

MEAH HEARINGTON ARAKAKI

—⬦—

One of the most memorable places of childhood may be found in your grandmother's kitchen. The smells, sounds, and tastes that came from that kitchen are all too great to describe in words. Perhaps it was a rich sensory experience set in the community of family: aunts, uncles, cousins, etc. For so many of us, our grandmother's spiritual gift of hospitality was manifested through her cooking; it was how she brought us together, how she loved us. Was that the case for you? If not, where is the preparation and consumption of food most prominent in your background?

Food is a central element of our existence and identity. It began at our creation when God gave Adam and Eve the ability to eat from any tree in the garden -- with one exception. At the fall, Adam and Eve took and ate from the one thing forbidden. Then in the New Testament we see Jesus as the Bread of Life and Living Water. Food is woven throughout our story. Whether you believe these passages to be literal or symbolic, the concept of eating is clearly central to our spiritual and physical existence.

Food is also a defining factor in every culture - how and what we eat. It is essential to each of our days. We are not able to exist long without being reminded of our need for nourishment. We gather together around food, and it is a conduit of community: we gather to partake both in spiritual nourishment through Holy Eucharist with brothers and sisters in Christ, and in daily physical nourishment with family and friends. However, as with Adam and Eve, the concept of receiving the gift of nourishment from God can be easily twisted to become us trying to obtain something that is not ours, that fills us in ways that counter our nourishment and health.

In Proverbs 9:17-18 (NIV), Lady Folly says to those passing by her house, "Stolen water is sweet; food eaten in secret is delicious!" Verse 18 then says, "But little do they know that the dead are there, that her guests are deep in the realm of the dead."

So how do we know if we are eating in the manner of Adam, Eve, and Lady Folly or as Jesus, reclining with those at the last supper? One brings death, dis-unity, and dis-ease. Adam and Eve, through "grasping," "taking," and "consuming" what was not theirs, created separation from each other and more importantly, between them and God. The other brings life, unity, health, and wholeness. Jesus breaks bread, pours himself out, and freely gives to those at his table. The disciples' response is to receive. By receiving the gift of food, we are brought nearer to the giver, nearer to those who partake with us, and nearer to our own wholeness. Just as a grandmother may give and love freely through her cooking, Jesus gives us our daily bread.

As you sit at table, as you receive into your own temple of Christ, may you eat for life, joy, community, and nourished wholeness. And may you savor the flavors that are the gifts of God.

"Do not work for the food that perishes, but for the food that endures to eternal life, which the Son of Man will give to you."
—John 6:27a (ESV)

"There is a symbiotic relationship - cross training, if you will - between the pleasures we find in gathered worship and those in my teacup or in a warm blanket or in the smell of bread baking."
—Tish Harrison Warren

COME AND DINE
A HYMN BY C.C. WIDMEYER, 1907

Jesus has a table spread
Where the saints of God are fed,
He invites His chosen people,
"Come and dine";
With His manna He doth feed
And supplies our every need:
Oh, 'tis sweet to sup with Jesus all the time!

Refrain:
"Come and dine," the Master calleth,
"Come and dine";
You may feast at Jesus' table
all the time;
He Who fed the multitude,
turned the water into wine,
To the hungry calleth now,
"Come and dine."

The disciples came to land,
Thus obeying Christ's command,
For the Master called unto them, "Come and dine";
There they found their heart's desire,
Bread and fish upon the fire;
Thus He satisfies the hungry every time. [Refrain]

Soon the Lamb will take His bride
To be ever at His side,
All the host of heaven will assembled be;

Oh, 'twill be a glorious sight,
All the saints in spotless white;
And with Jesus they will feast eternally. [Refrain]

REFLECTION QUESTIONS

When you think of your own relationship to food, which biblical character discussed previously best describes your own heart attitude toward food?

Are there any areas of sin in your life related to food? If so, can you take time to confess these to God and receive his gift of life?

What are you presently learning about the preparation and consumption of food and its impact on your physical and relational life in Christ?

What does it look like in your own life to eat in a way that brings life, community, nourishment, and wholeness? Are there practical ways that you can move from grasping at food to receiving nourishment? Allowing more time to savor your food? Eating with others instead of eating in secret? Prayerfully considering the gift in front of you before you eat?

SPIRITUAL PRACTICES

Prayerfully reflect and journal about your own practices of eating. What do your reflections reveal about your view of food?

Try having a meal alone with Jesus. Find a time to either prepare a meal or dine out with Jesus. Intentionally invite him to be present with you at the meal, then take your time, savor your food, notice ways that God has created your body to respond to food.

Plan a meal with others where you intentionally focus on how the food brings you together. Allow ample time to linger, to savor, to connect.

Engage in the practice of receiving from the Lord's Table in the Eucharist, then prayerfully reflect upon the experience.

Converse with others in your family and friendship circle about the importance of table fellowship and the delight that's created by shared preparation and enjoyment of meals, vibrant conversation around spiritual topics, and the resultant relationship and community that's built together. Notice the emotions this conversation evokes.

A Prayer of Illumination:
Lord Jesus Christ, the One who was broken and poured out for me, may You enable me to receive the gifts You have given. Grant that I may sit at Your table today and every day in thankfulness and consider the daily gift of food that nourishes us, both physically and spiritually. Amen.

9. SABBATH

JEREMY STEFANO

In the letter to the Hebrews it is stated that a promise of rest remains in the New Covenant. The writer was so concerned that these Hebrew Christians would miss this rest that he wrote: "... let us fear lest any of you should seem to have failed to reach it" (Hebrews 4:1 ESV). Apparently, they were in jeopardy of doing so, as Israel had failed to enter the Sabbath rest time and again.

God's intention of rest for his covenant people involved inhabiting the last day of the week in a way that was beyond the definition and constraints of their labors. Abraham Heschel explains from a Jewish perspective: "Six days a week we wrestle with the world, wringing profit from the earth; on the Sabbath we especially care for the seed of eternity planted in the soul." Since such is true for those under the Law, what of those who literally have the seed-life of the Spirit implanted in them? Should we not also fear lest we come short of cultivating what is within?

When Jesus called out, "Come to me all you who labor and are heavy laden. I will give you rest" (Matthew 11: 28) he was inviting all would-be disciples into a Sabbath life in which all carnal and worldly aspirations might be shed. He was beckoning his followers into a way of being present to others that did not involve asserting their own self-importance over those around them. Much labor is expended on getting ahead or at least at not getting left behind. Conditions in life are thorny, and people seem contrary or threatening. Consequently, we work at asserting ourselves and our own interests, trying to secure a self-styled place of significance or purpose.

Jesus' invitation, however, is to enter his Sabbath way of being in the world. "Learn from me," he said. "I am gentle and humble in heart, and you will find rest for your souls." In a relentless push-and-pull world, where self-protection and self-assertion appear to be the only way of survival, Jesus opens another way. It is his way of living at rest within, and at peace with all around him, secure in the calm assurance of the love of his Father.

This way of keeping Sabbath with Jesus will free up inner emotional resources that might have otherwise been used selfishly. Now those energies will be available for much more fruitful and loving ends. It requires that the disciple heed more completely the ways and promptings of that Spirit life within, preferring His leading over against the rush of the fleshly impulse.

There will then certainly be rest for the soul. It will have the quality of inner peace, the peace that only Jesus can give.

"God created us in his image. He is a God who works and then rests. When we rest, we honor the way God made us. Rest can be a spiritual act -- a truly human act of submission to and dependence on God who watches over all things as we rest."
— Adele Calhoun, Spiritual Disciplines Handbook

"Sabbath is time sanctified, time betrothed, time we perceive and receive and approach differently from all other time. Sabbath time is unlike every and any other time on the clock and the calendar. We are more intimate with it. We are more thankful for it. We are more protective of it and generous with it. We become more ourselves in the presence of Sabbath; more vulnerable, less afraid. More ready to confess, to be silent, to be small, to be valiant."
— Mark Buchanan, The Rest of God

JESUS, I AM RESTING, RESTING
A HYMN BY JEAN PIGOTT, 1876

Jesus! I am resting, resting, In the joy of what Thou art;
I am finding out the greatness of Thy loving heart.
Thou hast bid me gaze upon Thee, And Thy beauty fills my soul,
For, by Thy transforming power, Thou hast made me whole.

Refrain: Jesus! I am resting, resting, in the joy of what Thou art;
I am finding out the greatness of Thy loving heart.

Oh, how great Thy loving kindness, Vaster, broader than the sea:
Oh, how marvelous Thy goodness, Lavished all on me!
Yes, I rest in Thee, Beloved, Know what wealth of grace is Thine,
Know Thy certainty of promise, And have made it mine.

Jesus! I am resting, resting, in the joy of what Thou art;
I am finding out the greatness of Thy loving heart.

Simply trusting Thee, Lord Jesus, I behold Thee as Thou art,
And Thy love, so pure, so changeless, Satisfies my heart;
Satisfies its deepest longings, Meets, supplies its every need,
Compasseth me round with blessings, Thine is love indeed.

Jesus! I am resting, resting, in the joy of what Thou art;
I am finding out the greatness of Thy loving heart.

Ever lift Thy face upon me, As I work and wait for Thee;
Resting 'neath Thy smile, Lord Jesus, Earth's dark shadows flee.
Brightness of my Father's glory, Sunshine of my Father's face,
Keep me ever trusting, resting, Fill me with Thy grace.

Jesus! I am resting, resting, in the joy of what Thou art;
I am finding out the greatness of Thy loving heart.

REFLECTION QUESTIONS

In what ways do you labor to get ahead or strive toward not getting behind?

How might a false sense of identity be prohibiting you from truly resting and walking away from your labor?

In what areas of life do you see yourself exerting energy in self-assertion?

In a world of relentless grasping, self-preoccupation and endless productivity, how will you embrace Jesus' invitation into a restful, calm, and joy-filled way of life?

What are some daily, weekly, monthly, and annual rhythms that would foster deeper rest and renewal for your body and soul?

SPIRITUAL PRACTICES

"Cease from that which is necessary and embrace that which gives life."
(from Buchanan's Rest of God).

Take a nap. Brew a pot of tea. Enjoy a leisure walk through the woods. Listen to refreshing music.

Spend a day without the use of any technology (phone, computer, television, etc).

Offer thanksgiving and gratitude for the gifts present in your life.

Light a candle to signify this sacred, set-apart time for the re-creation of your soul.

Spend time in attentive, listening prayer. Ask God to renew your mind and body.

A Prayer of Illumination from the Book of Common Prayer:
"*For the Good Use of Leisure*"
God, in the course of this busy life, give us times of refreshment and peace; and grant that we may so use our leisure to rebuild our bodies and renew our minds, that our spirits may be opened to the goodness of your creation; through Jesus Christ our Lord. Amen.

10. REST

ADELE AHLBERG CALHOUN

—◈—

REST: "Busyness makes us stop caring about the things we care about." – Mark Buchanan

The 24/7 pressure to drive and strive rules every part of life – even weekends and vacations. Saturday and Sunday aren't for rest. It's time to catch up on more work! Work in the garden, wash the car, do the books, take the kids to games, go shopping. On vacation we stay plugged into laptops and keep earning our identity while we play. It's how we sustain the myth that we are indispensable. Overwork is our badge of honor. Christians reward over-working as much as anyone. And church leaders struggle to model alternatives to the work addictions that ruin families, damage souls, and sometimes kill us.

We are all devotees of the "Protestant work ethic." We like adages such as: The early bird catches the worm. ~ No pain, no gain. ~ Early to bed, early to rise makes a man healthy, wealthy and wise. ~ A penny saved is a penny earned. ~ Time is money. ~ There's no such thing as a free lunch. ~ Work won't kill you. ~ Do your best. ~ Never give up. ~The one with the most toys wins.

These bits of advice make us a productive nation. But they also make us a restless, driven, and exhausted people. Just because you choose your work doesn't mean you aren't a slave to it. We interact with a lot of slaves these days. Slaves have no Sabbath, no rest, no time off, no six- day work week, no reprieve. Slaves have to be productive even if it means working themselves sick or working themselves to death. If you cannot stop working, you aren't free – you are a slave with an income.

Rest is not laziness or a sign of lack of ambition. Rest is fundamental to God (Genesis 2: 2-3) and to the well-being of all creation. Rest is a transcendent anchor in the midst of doing. God wants us to rest because a society that encourages overwork is no different from a society that encourages lying, murder, stealing, and promiscuity. God also wants us to rest because if we don't, we will not have time to care about the people we love, the neighbors we know, the strangers we meet, and the gifts that come to us while we rest.

The ONE who holds the universe together by the power of his pinkie has a restful identity. An identity that is not derived from work alone. When our identity is derived only from producing, we push the envelope and deny our human limits. Jesus invites us to live unforced rhythms that honor both our talents and our vulnerabilities.

"Are you tired? Worn out? Burned out on religion? Come to me. Get away with me and you'll recover your life. I'll show you how to take a real rest. Walk with me and work with me – watch how I do it. Learn the unforced rhythms of grace. I won't lay anything heavy or ill-fitting on you. Keep company with me and you'll learn to live freely and lightly." —(Matthew 11. 28-30, *The Message*)

We need to lay our deadly doing down and taste the unforced rhythms of grace for ourselves. Receive the gift that keeps us from running on empty. Jesus knew when to say "no" to need so he could stay connected with God. He could resist the constant temptation to do something to prove who he was – because he was deeply at rest in who he was.

"...then because so many people were coming and going that they didn't
even have time to eat Jesus said, Come with me by yourselves to
a quiet place and get some rest."
—Mark 6:31

"Stopping touches the whole world with limits and it 'bears witness to whether or not
we have brought our habits and priorities in line with the ways and intentions of God.'"
—Norman Wirzba, Living the Sabbath

HOW SWEET IS MY REST
A HYMN BY BARNEY E. WARREN, 1893

How sweet is the comfort and rest of my soul,
Where peace doth so tranquilly flow;
Though storm-cloud and tempest and dark billows roll,
All my heart with His sunlight doth glow.

How sweet is my rest! And how richly I'm blest!
Oh, how sweet is the rest of my soul!

No fears shall alarm me though Satan be nigh,
He's subject to Jesus' control;
Though tempted and tried, Christ regardeth my cry,
Truly He is the joy of my soul.

How sweet is my rest! And how richly I'm blest!
Oh, how sweet is the rest of my soul!

REFLECTION QUESTIONS

How do you spend most of your "time off"? When and where do you most deeply rest?

What would a day of Sabbath rest look like in the ideal and in reality for you and yours?

Take a body inventory. What do your shoulders feel like? Your neck? Where do you hold tension in your body? What exhausts you? What is your body saying to you about your need for rest?

Listen deeply to what your body feels: headaches, passions, stiff neck, sweaty palms, likes and dislikes. Notice the butterflies in the stomach, the soft addictions, and the memories that play back in tapes we can't turn off. Bodies store memories that shape us. What memories keep you in slavery to earning an identity? Were you rewarded for not being who you are? Did you feel unwanted? Unworthy? Like you didn't belong?

SPIRITUAL PRACTICES

We may feel we can't take time for rest. Look for a few hours in the next week to honor your need to rest. Design a perfect day (or several hours) of rest and recreation for yourself. What do you include? What do you exclude? Who can help you schedule it?

Make a list of things you delight in (things like a nap, exercise, coffee with a friend, listening to music). As you do these things, be intentional about receiving the rest and renewal they can bring you. Thank God for the gift of rest.

Choose something to rest your body, something to rest your mind, and something to rest your soul this week.

Read a book on Sabbath rest. Consider teaching what you learn, and engage others in your community in conversation about incorporating Sabbath rest into your weekly lifestyle.

A Prayer of Illumination:
Lord, you are the God who works and rests. I am made in your image. Help me live into your unforced rhythms of grace. Give me courage to lay my deadly doing down and lean back into your arms and rest. Amen.

11. GRATITUDE

STEPHEN A. MACCHIA

$\diamondsuit$

Two friends meet regularly for coffee in a local restaurant in the center of the town where they live. Each time they visit this location, they are greeted by Danny behind the counter. When they head to their table each week, they're always chuckling about a quip that came from Danny as he took their order. They deeply appreciate Danny's service. One day theychose to tell him how grateful they were for his smile and witty sense of humor. His response? "Oh no, I'm going to blush." As Danny walked away with a sheepish grin and a red face, those few words of thanks became a simple gift of grace to one who's often taken for granted.

In this world filled with gripes, gossip, and guesswork in relationships, saying an occasional "thank you" is good for one's soul. In the words of Ann Voskamp (author of *One Thousand Gifts*), "Thanksgiving creates abundance." That rings true, and yet it's often forgotten. Gratitude is the gateway that leads all involved into a wide open space of grace and goodness. What better gift can we offer to God and others than the gift of gratitude?

N.T. Wright affirms the importance of gratitude as a Christian by reminding us, "When we learn to read the story of Jesus and see it as the story of the love of God, doing for us what we could not do for ourselves – that insight produces, again and again, a sense of astonished gratitude which is very near the heart of authentic Christian experience." As Christ followers, our gratitude comes from the heart of God, evidenced toward us in creation, in life itself, and in the outstretched arms of love that were extended redemptively on the cross in our behalf. The gift of our salvation is to be received in like fashion… with outstretched arms of humble gratitude.

> "To be grateful is to recognize the Love of God in everything He has given us - and He has given us everything. Every breath we draw is a gift of His love, every moment of existence is a grace, for it brings with it immense graces from Him. Gratitude therefore takes nothing for granted, is never unresponsive, is constantly awakening to new wonder and to praise of the goodness of God. For the grateful person knows that God is good, not by hearsay but by experience. And that is what makes all the difference." —Thomas Merton

When we see all of life as a gift from the hand of the Creator God, we develop a responsiveness to all things – good or hard – with an attitude of gratitude. Gratitude heals the broken heart, it brings together the divided home, and it bridges any relational gap before us. Gratitude strengthens the bonds of love between us and our worship of God, within our marriages and families, among our friendships, and even in the core of our personal sense of wellbeing. To be grateful rather than critical, thankful rather than cynical, and glad-hearted rather than bitter-minded, is to be filled to overflowing with an abundance that sustains all of life.

Will you offer today the gift of gratitude to another? If so, you will contribute to a life of abundance preferred by God Himself, and received with joy by all who are touched by the generosity of your heart.

"You say, 'If I had a little more, I should be very satisfied.' You make a mistake. If you are not content with what you have, you would not be satisfied if it were doubled."
— C.H. Spurgeon, The Spurgeon Series

"When it comes to life the critical thing is whether you take things for granted or take them with gratitude."
—G.K. Chesterton

PRAISE, MY SOUL, THE KING OF HEAVEN
WORDS BY HENRY FRANCIS LYTE, 1834

Praise, my soul, the King of heaven,
To his feet thy tribute bring;
Ransomed, healed, restored, forgiven,
Who like me his praise should sing?
Alleluia! Alleluia!
Praise the everlasting King.

Praise him for his grace and favour
To our fathers in distress;
Praise him still the same as ever,
Slow to chide, and swift to bless:
Alleluia! Alleluia!
Glorious in his faithfulness.

Father-like, he tends and spares us,
Well our feeble frame he knows;
In his hands he gently bears us,
Rescues us from all our foes:
Alleluia! Alleluia!
Widely as his mercy flows.

Angels, help us to adore him;
Ye behold him face to face;
Sun and moon, bow down before him,
Dwellers all in time and space:
Alleluia! Alleluia!
Praise with us the God of grace.

REFLECTION QUESTIONS

How can you begin to cultivate a heart of gratitude, focusing on abundance rather than scarcity?

Are there things/relationships in your life that are fueling negativity, cynicism, or grumbling? What steps might you take to confront these things/relationships with gratitude instead of complaint?

Is there an experience or event from your past (or in the present) that is cultivating bitterness or discontent? Ask God to reveal this to you. Seek his forgiveness, and determine steps you can take to move forward with gratitude and contentment.

Ask yourself, "Am I growing in gratitude?" once a week for the span of a month. Are you cultivating a heart of gratitude?

SPIRITUAL PRACTICES

Write a letter to a friend, mentor, or family member giving thanks for their presence in your life.

Giving thanks for how you've been blessed, consider a way in which you can extend material or financial generosity toward someone in need.

Begin a gratitude journal today. Make note of the gifts from today that evoke a thankful heart.

When you commune with God in prayer, be sure to begin with praise and gratitude. Avoid the temptation to move directly into petition or confession.

Gather a handful of Scripture passages, poems, lyrics, or quotes that help center your mind and heart on thankfulness and gratitude. Write these in your journal and place them where they can be seen.

A Prayer of Illumination:
Accept, O Lord, my thanks and praise for all that you have done. I thank you for the splendor of the whole creation, for the beauty of this world, for the wonder of life, and for the mystery of your love. You've lavished gift upon gift and blessing upon blessing. And I joyfully offer back my life to you in devotion and praise. I gratefully give you all praise, honor, and glory. Amen.

12. RULE OF LIFE

STEPHEN A. MACCHIA

$\diamond$

God has put a unique thumbprint on your life. He loves you so much that he has purposefully fashioned only one of you. And your Heavenly Father has planted deep within you God-given roles, gifts, passions, vision, and mission. In addition to your unique thumbprint, God has given you a one-of-a-kind footprint. Your footprint is the legacy and impact you leave on the world, how you carry out the unique particularities of life that God has lovingly invited you to fulfill. As Frederick Buechner has disclosed: it's the place where your deep gladness meets the hunger of the world.

What is a personal rule of life? It is a holistic description of the Spirit-empowered rhythms and relationships that create, redeem, sustain, and transform the life God invites you to humbly fulfill for Christ's glory. To discover your rule of life, begin by answering two fundamental questions: First, what is my unique thumbprint (roles, gifts, desires, vision, and mission)? And second, what is my unique footprint (spiritual, relational, physical, financial, and missional priorities)?

Sitting with the biblical text and considering these questions takes time and prayer-filled effort. Discerning one's thumbprint and footprint in this life are not instantaneous discoveries. Instead, these questions are carefully and deliberately explored in the context of one's faith community. After answering these questions that frame one's rule of life, forming one's rule of life includes all the major areas of particularity that define our daily journey both descriptively and prescriptively.

Consider prayerfully your spiritual, relational, physical, financial, and missional priorities. Looking at each of these areas one at a time will help weave together a personal rule of life that engages all the senses and brings to life all major areas of personal development. God's invitation in each of these areas is what we need to listen for, and then we can respond to the initiatives of the Spirit in every regard. Here, it's important to interview the Lord and seek His face in the primary places of personal and spiritual growth. And recognize that along the way these specifics will be modified according to life circumstances and new realities.

Fulfilling a personal rule of life happens in the context of Christian community. We don't fully understand or embrace our rule of life in isolation. We need our spiritual friends and faith communities to affirm, celebrate, and enhance the living out of our rule for the honor and glory of God and His collective call to all of us in building up His Kingdom and strengthening His Church. This is the invitation to the well-ordered way: a way of life that re-orders our loves and re-defines our priorities that keep us focused on loving and serving God. Discover the wonderful ways in which God has uniquely created you with a special thumbprint. And may you respond with a growing desire to fulfill your particular footprint for faithful daily living. Embrace this opportunity with joy and gladness of heart, soul, mind, and strength!

"You make known to me the path of life; you will fill me with joy in your presence,
with eternal pleasures at your right hand."
—Psalm 16:11

"So, here's what I want you to do, God helping you: Take your everyday, ordinary
life—your sleeping, eating, going-to-work, and walking-around life—and place it
before God as an offering. Embracing what God does for you is the best thing you can
do for him. Don't become so well-adjusted to your culture that you fit into it without
even thinking. Instead, fix your attention on God. You'll be changed from the inside
out. Readily recognize what he wants from you, and quickly respond to it. Unlike the
culture around you, always dragging you down to its level of immaturity, God brings
the best out of you, develops well-formed maturity in you."
—Romans 12:1-2, The Message

FILL THOU MY LIFE
A HYMN BY HORATIUS BONAR, 1866

Fill Thou my life, O Lord my God, In every part with praise.
That my whole being may proclaim, Thy being and Thy ways.
Not for the lip of praise alone, Nor e'en the praising heart I ask.
But for a life made up, Of praise in every part!

Praise in the common words I speak, Life's common looks and tones.
In fellowship in hearth and board, With my beloved ones.
Not in the temple crowd alone, Where holy voices chime.
But in the silent paths of earth, The quiet rooms of time.

Fill every part of me with praise, Let all my being speak
Of Thee and of Thy love, O Lord, Poor though I be, and weak.
So shalt Thou, Lord, from me, e'en me, Receive the glory due.
And so shall I begin on earth, The song forever new.

So shall each fear, each fret, each care, Be turned into a song
And every winding of the way, The echo shall prolong.
So shall no part of day or night, From sacredness be free.
But all my life, in every step, Be fellowship with Thee.

REFLECTION QUESTIONS

Give thanks for the privilege of being a beloved child of God. In what ways has the Lord blessed your life?

Define the places in your life that need some readjustment. What loves need to be re-ordered and appropriately re-aligned around God's priorities?

Though your life may seem full, does it at times feel unfulfilling and empty? What contributes to those feelings?

Are your present practices (rhythms and relationships) "right" for you? How might God be calling you to adjust your present priorities?

How can you encourage others in their pursuit of a personal rule of life?

SPIRITUAL PRACTICES

Offer your gratitude to the Lord today by freely sharing a word of encouragement to a special friend.

Pray for wisdom and courage to look prayerfully at all aspects of your life: roles, gifts, passion, vision, and mission.

Write down the roles you fulfill today and the primary relationships within each role. Assess the health of each.

Write out a condensed spiritual autobiography, noting the times when you were most aware/unaware of God (i.e., experiences, seasons, joys, disappointment).

Note the ways God is leading you to review your spiritual, relational, physical, financial, and missional priorities. Write out the top 1-3 ways you can refocus these priorities during this season of life.

A Prayer of Illumination:
Thank you, Lord, for how you have uniquely fashioned my life. Help me live into the rhythms that you are inviting me into as your beloved child. Enable me to live fully in the gifts you have generously given to me, and may I steward them with wisdom and joy. Illuminate the path and enlighten my heart, that I may offer my life in daily service to you and to others. In the name of Christ, Amen.

13. REORDERING LOVES

STEPHEN A. MACCHIA

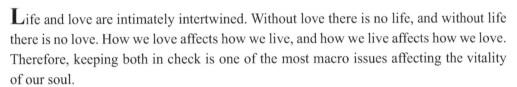

Life and love are intimately intertwined. Without love there is no life, and without life there is no love. How we love affects how we live, and how we live affects how we love. Therefore, keeping both in check is one of the most macro issues affecting the vitality of our soul.

Jonathan Edwards (1703-1758), one of if not America's greatest theologian, preached and wrote about our Affections: those deeply held desires which take root in our hearts and souls and which govern our feelings and aspirations for God, our lives with others, our world, and our inner selves. Centuries before Edwards, St. Augustine (354-430 A.D.) recognized that as we love in our hearts, so we are in our essence as people of God. And, the more we foster ungodly or unholy affections, so too will our love(s) be disordered and our lives out of sync with God's priorities for us.

In every respect, we are governed by our affections…toward people, possessions, powers, and persuasions that reign supreme in our hearts. Our affections are our deeply held desires, which are given to us by God and are to be devoted to godly pursuits in our lives. But, in our sinful state as human beings, we allow other affections to take hold of our heart's longings. And it's these disordered loves which need to be assessed and realigned toward God alone. Otherwise, we will live unholy lives. When we reorder our loves, we likewise reorder our lives.

Will you reorder your love for People? Our primary relationships with family, friends, even our pets need to be held in proper perspective. Relationships, as significant as they are to our lives, can become idols in our hearts and can trump our primary love for God.

Will you reorder your love for Possessions? The things we believe we worked hard for and deserve to own, including all of our tangible items, our financial portfolios, and even our titles, degrees, and other signs of our human stature in society, must be held loosely. The tighter the grip we have on them, the firmer the hold they have on us.

Will you reorder your love for Power? When it's more important that we win the race, conquer the prize, control the outcome, manipulate others, even hold to the attitudes and convictions we believe in firmly, then these things have become more dominant than they should be. Willingly cooperating, rather than competing with others, will create an atmosphere of growth for all.

Will you reorder your love for Persuasions? As our temptations tantalize us and our feelings take over wisdom, when addictions consume the mind and technology supplants relationships, those persuasive elements from our culture (and from the enemy of our souls) need laser-focus elimination. Otherwise, all such persuasions will trigger the will and lead us down unhealthy, unwholesome pathways.

The reordering of our loves will take a lifetime to accomplish. It's only possible as we submit to the loving will of God, entrust our hearts into the Father's faithful hands, and remain empowered by the Spirit of God, in order for us to daily live and love as Jesus invites us as his beloved disciples. May it be so in your heart and life today.

"My love is my weight: wherever I go my love is what brings me there."
—Augustine, Confessions, 13.9

"God cannot give us a happiness and peace apart from Himself,
because it is not there. There is no such thing."
—C.S. Lewis

TAKE MY LIFE AND LET IT BE
A HYMN BY FRANCES R. HAVERGAL, 1874

Take my life and let it be consecrated, Lord, to Thee.
Take my moments and my days. Let them flow in endless praise.

Take my hands and let them move at the impulse of Thy love.
Take my feet and let them be swift and beautiful for Thee.

Take my voice and let me sing always, only for my King.
Take my lips and let them be filled with messages from Thee.

Take my silver and my gold. Not a mite would I withhold.
Take my intellect and use every pow'r as Thou shalt choose.

Take my will and make it Thine. It shall be no longer mine.
Take my heart, it is Thine own. It shall be Thy royal throne.

Take my love, my Lord, I pour at Thy feet its treasure store.
Take myself and I will be ever, only, all for Thee.

REFLECTION QUESTIONS

People: Who has an unhealthy grip on your heart today? Open your hands and release them into God's tender loving care.

Possessions: What do you own that you need instead to steward? Consider being generous to a fault with what you possess.

Power: What area of life do you dominate in order to control? Prayerfully invite others to speak into your propensity to win.

Persuasions: How has the enemy of your soul tantalized you and led you outside the will of God? Confess it and be set free.

SPIRITUAL PRACTICES

People: Write a page-long prayer in your journal about the desired quality of your primary relationships.

Possessions: Give away something that you treasure to another person or cause anonymously this coming week.

Power: Relinquish the need to win your next disagreement. Instead, simply listen and only respond in prayer.

Persuasions: Identify the one temptation that continues to tug your heart and pull you into (potential) disobedience. Ask God for healing and grace.

A Prayer of Illumination:
Lord of my heart, I invite you to rearrange and reorder my affections so that my loves are focused on what you love most and my life is directed toward your eternal abundance and joy. In your perfect love, Father, Son, and Holy Spirit. Amen.

14. PERSONAL RETREAT

DIANA CURREN BENNETT

Driving into the retreat center for your first silent retreat can be anxiety-producing. What does one "do" during this time? Your comfort zone may be more focused on studying and exegeting biblical texts, feeding head knowledge, working on projects and meeting deadlines. It's easier to consider staying active on retreat rather than resting, reading, praying, and actually doing less rather than more. For many, there's great uncertainty about taking a retreat, especially if it's a silent retreat. You may have spent a whole hour in silence before, but 36 hours? What will a silent personal retreat entail?

Taking a personal retreat, especially one that includes lots of silence and solitude, is not the most popular way to spend a day, overnight or weekend. But, over the years, countless believers have found these to be some of the most life-defining moments in their spiritual journey. Mostly because the fruit of silence and surrender to God is evidenced in transformation. The change that occurs in one's heart and soul on retreat is unparalleled. Here on retreat we press the pause button of our rushed, chaotic, and noisy lives in order to listen more attentively to God in his Word, in nature, in prayer, in worship, and in reflection.

For many, it takes practice to learn how best to experience a silent retreat. Feeling a bit unsettled and anxious is normal. Many wonder if they will indeed hear from God.

They are unsure about how best to spend their time, and yet they are encompassed with a desire to experience deep communion with Jesus. There is great joy to be experienced in this unique encounter that only God can orchestrate.

What is it that tugs on your soul toward silence with God but then fears what will happen when you finally get there? What do you expect to experience? Initially, many will come overly prepared for boredom by loading the car with various books to read or projects to complete. As experience mounts, one will bring nothing but a Bible and journal on retreat. Silence. Recognizing God's voice. Reflection. Confession. Praise. Enjoying my sacred pathways in nature. Resting in his arms. Feeling loved beyond understanding. These are the fruit one can experience when we are unencumbered by the trappings of busyness, noisiness, and the normal chaos of our lives.

We come into a silent retreat seeking God's face. This spacious time offers the gift of a deeper knowledge of God and ourselves in light of his Word. We come to ask for guidance and spiritual discernment, God's wisdom and counsel in times of uncertainty. We come into God's presence to rest. To climb up into our Father's lap to be loved and restored. We come to praise God for his presence in desolation and consolation. We come, perhaps, to listen to music that connects our soul to his love, to hear the sounds of his creation and receive restorative rest in the quietness of our surroundings.

A personal retreat offers us two special gifts: silence and a radically simplified environment. Stepping away from all the chaotic stimuli of life invites simplicity and clarity. And entering into silence leaves us open and vulnerable. The retreat environment provides this so beautifully. It is a powerful experience to spend time in a place where prayers have previously soaked the walls and graced the landscape.

Are silence and simplicity the sum and total purpose of a retreat? Surely not! God calls us to be restored, spend time with him, confess our sins, and ask for guidance in areas of our life that need his help and direction. The challenge is to enter quietness and stillness long enough to hear what God wants to share with us.

As you enter the driveway of a favorite retreat house, let busyness, chaos, and anxiety slip away. Silence and simplicity will greet you like a faithful friend and accompany you into God's loving presence.

"Come with me by yourselves to a quiet place and get some rest."
—Mark 6:31

"I have found real value in thinking of retreat as the quiet in-the-moment seizing of opportunities occasioned by unexpected intrusions of God's Spirit."
—Larry Crabb

TAKE TIME TO BE HOLY
A HYMN BY WILLIAM D. LONGSTAFF, 1882

Take time to be holy,
speak oft with thy Lord;
Abide in Him always,
and feed on His Word.
Make friends of God's children,
help those who are weak,
Forgetting in nothing
His blessing to seek.

Take time to be holy,
the world rushes on;
Spend much time in secret,
with Jesus alone.
By looking to Jesus,
like Him thou shalt be;
Thy friends in thy conduct
His likeness shall see.

Take time to be holy,
let Him be thy Guide;
And run not before Him,
whatever betide.
In joy or in sorrow,
still follow the Lord,
And, looking to Jesus,
still trust in His Word.

Take time to be holy,
be calm in thy soul,
Each thought and each motive

beneath His control.
Thus led by His Spirit
to fountains of love,
Thou soon shalt be fitted
for service above.

REFLECTION QUESTIONS

Ask yourself, "What do I need from God right now?" Perhaps the answer is rest, or love, or direction, or simply being spiritually restored, basking in God's Word and presence and listening for his tender voice.

Upon hearing or sensing what is best for you at this time, you might journal your thoughts as a way of exploring what God is saying to you. What is God inviting you to notice in this spacious day together?

What distractions will potentially stand in the way of your prayerfulness, silence, and rest? Name the distractions and ask God to help you release them into his loving hands as you retreat.

Upon the conclusion of your retreat, what is the "take away" for you? You might focus on your loved ones, daily responsibilities, and current life circumstances. Ask God to give you a heart of acceptance, joy, patience, and an extra measure of love for the place in life to which he has called you.

SPIRITUAL PRACTICES

On retreat, take a walk and transition yourself from the busyness of life into a more relaxed, quiet, attentive, and refreshing mindset.

Find a quiet place to be alone. Read Psalm 139. As this Scripture leads you into opening up to God, surrender your time and in stillness listen for his voice.

Try a "palms down; palms up" releasing prayer. In recognizing the issues that might be pressing in on you, place your palms down on your knees and list the many concerns. Offer them up to God by turning your palms up. Release those to him while being open and receptive to issues that God might bring to your attention.

Are you in need of rest? You might practice the art of the retreat nap--yes, this is both allowed and encouraged! A rested soul is a more reflective and receptive soul.

Look ahead in your calendar and plan now for your next retreat. Don't let too much time pass between these sacred encounters with the living God.

A Prayer of Illumination:
I pray that you, being rooted and established in love, may have power, together with all the Lord's holy people, to grasp how wide and long and high and deep is the love of Christ, and to know this love that surpasses knowledge – that you may be filled to the measure of all the fullness of God. (Ephesians 3:17-19)

15. PRAYING THE PSALMS

TED WUESTE

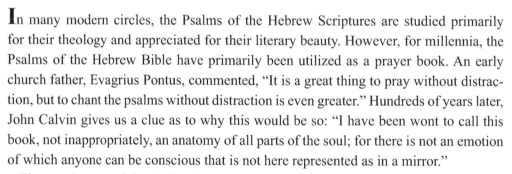

In many modern circles, the Psalms of the Hebrew Scriptures are studied primarily for their theology and appreciated for their literary beauty. However, for millennia, the Psalms of the Hebrew Bible have primarily been utilized as a prayer book. An early church father, Evagrius Pontus, commented, "It is a great thing to pray without distraction, but to chant the psalms without distraction is even greater." Hundreds of years later, John Calvin gives us a clue as to why this would be so: "I have been wont to call this book, not inappropriately, an anatomy of all parts of the soul; for there is not an emotion of which anyone can be conscious that is not here represented as in a mirror."

The true beauty of the Psalms is that they express what we are often not able to put into words for ourselves. The intricacies of our hearts, which are often mysterious and frequently fearful to us, are ground which is not tread often enough. The Psalms invite us to explore and express our hearts so that God can shape and form us in the context of relationship with himself.

Some psalms express a deep desire for God (e.g., "as the deer pants ..." Ps 42) which draws out the deepest, truest parts of who we are. We might feel timid to pray such lofty things or might not even be "in touch" with these profound desires, but the psalms prod us in this direction. In addition, some psalms express views of God which are not correct per se, but are reflective of our human condition. The imprecatory psalms, for example, often speak of desiring vengeance (Ps 137:9), and the lament psalms frequently speak of seeing God as one who has forgotten us (Ps 13). God is not threatened by our inaccurate thoughts and perceptions. He desires that we come as we are. The Psalms model this approach and beckon us to do the same.

And, rather than simply seeing the Psalms according to theological categories (e.g., praise psalms, Messianic psalms, or lament psalms), it can be helpful to see them based on what is happening in the soul of the one who is praying. Walter Brueggeman suggests that the Psalms can be categorized by "season of the soul," represented by times of Orientation, Disorientation, and Reorientation. Especially in times of disorientation, it can be difficult to pray, and psalms that reflect this season can carry us along.

The Psalms gives us permission to be in process and transition. Far too often, we can feel the pressure of needing to "parrot" good theology. But the Psalms encourage us to express the real us – those parts of us which doubt, feel anger, or experience confusion, disappointment, or darkness.

So, praying the Psalms can draw out our hearts, give voice to particular seasons, and give courage to live into these seasons, all the while growing in intimacy with Godand entrusting our formation to him. Additionally, while we may not be in a particular season ourselves, we are nudged to identify with those who are in such a place.

"Why are you cast down, O my soul, and why are you in turmoil within me?
Hope in God; for I shall again praise him, my salvation."
—Psalm 42:5 (ESV)

"This is pure grace that God tells us how we can speak with him
and have fellowship with him."
—Dietrich Bonhoeffer, Psalms: The Prayer Book of the Bible

OH, SAFE TO THE ROCK THAT IS HIGHER THAN I
A HYMN BY WILLIAM ORCUTT CUSHING, 1876

Oh, safe to the Rock that is higher than I,
My soul in its conflicts and sorrows would fly,
So sinful, so weary, Thine, Thine would I be,
Thou blest Rock of Ages, I'm hiding in Thee.

Refrain:
Hiding in Thee, Hiding in Thee,
Thou Blest Rock of Ages, I'm Hiding in Thee

In the calm of the noontide, in sorrow's lone hour,
In times when temptation casts o'er me its power;
In the tempests of life, on its wide, heaving sea,
Thou blest Rock of Ages, I'm hiding in Thee.

How oft in the conflict, when pressed by the foe,
I have fled to my Refuge and breathed out my woe,
How often, when trials like sea-billows roll,
Have I hidden in Thee, O Thou Rock of my soul.

REFLECTION QUESTIONS

At the present time, which season (winter, spring, summer, or fall) is most representative of my soul? How is this manifest?

Which psalms might best reflect honest prayers during this season of my soul?

Are there any psalms to which I am resistant? To what might this resistance relate?

Are there any psalms which make my heart leap with desire, anticipation, or longing?

What might this be saying about the state of my soul?

In what way can I encourage others to pray the Psalms in their devotional practice?

SPIRITUAL PRACTICES

Simply take a psalm and pray the words as they are.

Select a psalm. Read through it and get a feel. Go back through and pray the psalm slowly, stopping at places to meditate and sit with the words.

Paraphrase a psalm, putting the words into your own words with your own experiences as the descriptors.

Pray through the Psalms over a one-month period. Pray through five psalms each day in whatever way you feel led.

Memorize a few key psalms that you will be able to recite as prompted by the Spirit throughout the day.

A Prayer of Illumination:
Gracious Father, give me the courage to engage you honestly from my heart. Thank you for receiving me right where I am, that I might know you in the realities of my life. I entrust myself to You, believing that You will shape me and guide me according to Your grace and holiness. Amen.

POSTURES

16. SILENCE AND SOLITUDE

MATT SCOTT

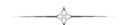

Though difficult to admit, let's be honest and face it—we are addicted to noise. It's incredibly challenging to spend an hour in the car without dialing up a friend or turning on the radio. And at home, we bombard ourselves with countless mediums of noise. Have you ever found the television blaring in the family room while music is playing through a kitchen stereo...at the same time you are talking on the phone with a distant relative? Or perhaps you're like many others and you find it difficult to be anywhere without your close companion, the smart phone. Our reality is such that our lives are filled to overflowing with noise and distractions. And if we pay close attention, we see our tendency to fill life's moments with music, television, email, internet, and conversation rather than sitting quietly in a place of unhurried silence.

So, ask yourself this question: How is the noise of my life drowning out the voice of God?

Often we are too hurried to spend alone time with God. Many have called this a "quiet time," while others may consider it a "prayer closet" or "devotional time." Regardless, it is most important that these sacred times include the rhythms of silence and solitude. In silence, we quiet both external and internal noises so we can be fully present to God. And in solitude, we intentionally separate from others so we can be attentive to the

Triune God. Isn't it true that our fear of being alone drives us toward more activity and noise? Thus, when we purpose to be still and engage in silence and solitude, we learn what it means to be a human- being rather than a human-doing.

Christ Jesus lived out these rhythms, regularly seeking a solitary place where he could be alone with the Father. Amidst his earthly ministry of teaching, healing, performing miracles, and making disciples, Jesus modeled a life of silence and solitude (see Mt. 4:1-11, Mk. 1:35, Lk. 6:12, Mt. 14:23, Lk. 5:16, Mt. 17:1-9). And we, too, are invited to follow his example.

The disciplines of silence and solitude will open the door for deeper intimacy with God. So, let the Lord invite you to spend some unhurried, uncluttered, spacious time with him. Leave behind any agenda or hopes of discovering some marvelous strategy for fixing your life. Simply sit quietly and alone with the Holy One. Listen carefully for his tender, loving voice. Embrace fully all that God desires to do in you as you sit quietly and patiently before him.

"We are so afraid of silence that we chase ourselves from one event to the next in order not to have to spend a moment alone with ourselves, i n order not to have to look at ourselves in the mirror."
—Dietrich Bonhoeffer, Meditating on the Word

"Attentiveness to God's Spirit requires deeply receptive, prayerful listening. Practicing the art of attending to the Spirit involves us in contemplative listening. Such listening is quite distinct from the various ways in which we generally listen to another ... it is holy listening, rooted in silence. It seeks emptiness in order to be filled with the Spirit. It is permeated by humility. Such listening assumes that the Spirit is active among us and works through us. It is primarily receptive, patient, watchful, and waiting. Yet it does not fear action when action is called for." –
—Wendy Wright, Companions in Christ: Participant's Book, Part 5

BE STILL MY SOUL
A HYMN BY KATHARINA A. von SCHLEGEL

Be still, my soul: the Lord is on thy side.
Bear patiently the cross of grief or pain.
Leave to thy God to order and provide;
In every change, He faithful will remain.
Be still, my soul: thy best, thy heavenly Friend
Through thorny ways leads to a joyful end.

Be still, my soul: thy God doth undertake
To guide the future, as He has the past.
Thy hope, thy confidence let nothing shake;
All now mysterious shall be bright at last.
Be still, my soul: the waves and winds still know
His voice who ruled them while He dwelt below.

Be still, my soul: the hour is hastening on
When we shall be forever with the Lord.
When disappointment, grief and fear are gone,
Sorrow forgot, love's purest joys restored.
Be still, my soul: when change and tears are past
All safe and blessèd we shall meet at last.

Be still, my soul: begin the song of praise
On earth, believing, to Thy Lord on high;

REFLECTION QUESTIONS

Are you fearful of being silent/alone? Is that curious to you? What might be behind your fear?

How much time each day do you carve out for silence?

What do you sense God is saying to you in the midst of your silence and solitude?

What things are distracting you from hearing the voice of the Lord?

How do you want to embrace silence and solitude on a more consistent basis?

SPIRITUAL PRACTICES

Set aside at least ten minutes each day for silence. Breathe deeply and become aware of God's presence. Afterwards, journal about your experience.

Designate a "sacred space" in your home where you can retreat into silence and solitude.

Drive to work without talking on your phone or turning on the radio.

Spend an entire day without the use of technology (computer, iPhone, iPad).

Notice your emotional response(s) to time spent alone. Journal your feelings.

A Prayer of Illumination:

May my soul be stilled in your presence; free me from my propensity to fill my life with noise. And enable me to fully embrace the joy of simply being with you, loving Father. Amen.

17. HUMILITY

KEVIN ANTLITZ

Throughout church history, humility is traditionally what Christians have focused on during Lent. Ash Wednesday marks the start of the forty-day Lenten journey and begins with the humbling reminder: "Remember you are dust and to dust you shall return." As we embark on this journey each year, we are invited to enter more deeply into the practice of humility. But humility isn't just for Lent; it's for each day of our life in Christ.

It's important to remember what humility is not. To be made of dust is actually not so bad. We read in Genesis that "the Lord God formed the man of dust from the ground..." and proceeds with the benediction that all that he made was "very good." Our trouble really lies with the second reminder: "To dust you shall return." In a word, our problem, our plight is death – the result of sin, inspired by pride. The ultimate cure is found in humility alone – in Christ's humbling himself to take on flesh and then death on a cross, and our humbling ourselves to receive his death on our behalf by faith (Philippians 2). Christ's condescending to our low estate is what enables our own exaltation in Christ – if only we have the humility to receive it.

Humility is not about self-loathing; rather, humility includes an acknowledgment and an action. First, as an acknowledgment, it means that we accept our reality: we are sinners decisively saved by grace once for all, but we also continually sin and continually need grace. Lent, therefore, provides an opportunity to take an honest look in the mirror without make-up and without pretension. It's an opportunity to allow light to shine in the unexposed places we try to hide from God and others. The purpose is not a heightened sense of guilt and shame but healing, renewal, and freedom.

Second, humility is also an action. Once we take a hard look in the mirror, we are invited into confession and repentance with the hope and expectation of healing and renewal. Humbly loving and serving others in Jesus' name is the fruit of a life in pursuit of humility and contentment.

In the coming days, embrace the hard work of acknowledging your reality and take action to grow in your intimacy with Christ. The emphasis is not on what we've done wrong but on being made right again. Humility depends not on considering oneself to be worthless but in resting securely in our being loved more deeply by a loving Father than our very deepest sins can go. That is why, according to Chesterton, "It is always the secure who are humble." If we cannot confess our deepest sins, perhaps it is because we are insecure in God's love. If this be true, thank God that you recognize it – there is no better place to begin.

May you be courageous in your self-reflection, honest in your confession, and faithful in your repentance. May this pursuit of humility and grace result in a greater sense of devotion and love for the resurrected Christ.

"Be wretched and mourn and weep. Let your laughter be turned to mourning and your joy to gloom. Humble yourselves before the Lord, and he will exalt you."
—James 4:9-10

"Humility is the bloom and the beauty of holiness. The chief mark of counterfeit holiness is its lack of humility."
—Andrew Murray, Humility: The Beauty of Holiness

"The fruit of the knowledge of truth is humility."
—Bernard of Clairvaux, The Steps of Humility and Pride

JESUS, I COME TO THEE
A HYMN BY WILLIAM SLEEPER, 1819-1904.

Out of my bondage, sorrow and night,
Jesus, I come; Jesus I come.
Into Thy freedom, gladness and light,
Jesus, I come to Thee.

Out of my sickness into Thy health,
Out of my wanting and into Thy wealth,
Out of my sin and into Thyself,
Jesus, I come to Thee.

Out of my shameful failure and loss,
Jesus, I come; Jesus, I come.
Into the glorious gain of Thy cross,
Jesus, I come to Thee.

Out of earth's sorrows into Thy balm,
Out of life's storms and into Thy calm,
Out of distress into jubilant psalm,
Jesus, I come to Thee.

Out of unrest and arrogant pride,
Jesus, I come; Jesus, I come.
Into Thy blessed will to abide,
Jesus, I come to Thee.

Out of myself to dwell in Thy love,
Out of despair into raptures above,
Upward forever on wings like a dove,
Jesus, I come to Thee.

Out of the fear and dread of the tomb,
Jesus, I come; Jesus, I come.
Into the joy and light of Thy home,
Jesus, I come to Thee.

Out of the depths of ruin untold,
Into the peace of Thy sheltering fold,
Ever Thy glorious face to behold,
Jesus, I come to Thee.

REFLECTION QUESTIONS

Use Psalm 51 to guide your prayers of confession. Let this be your prayer to God. What attitudes does this psalm evoke in your personal prayers?

In what ways have you sinned against God, your neighbor, or yourself in thought, word, or deed; in what you've done or left undone? Confess these things to the Lord, ask for His forgiveness, and repent.

What is one thing you are glad that people do not know about you (habit, addiction, attitude)? Confess this to the Lord, ask for his forgiveness, and repent.

With humility as a focus of your self-reflection in the coming days, how is God inviting you to pray humbly, speak humbly, and act humbly?

SPIRITUAL PRACTICES

Exhale = Confession

>   Agree with God about your sin (be specific) and confess to a trusted friend, if willing
>   (James 5:16)
>
>   Repent

Inhale = Appropriation

>   Receive his Spirit anew (Ephesians 5:18)
>
>   Receive his promise of forgiveness and cleansing (1 John 1:9)

Ask a trusted friend's perspective on an area of your life he/she thinks needs amending.

Reflect on the life of the most humble person you have known (in person or in history) and write out the attributes that express their humility. Consider ways to embody these traits yourself.

A Prayer of Illumination:

Search me, O God, and know my thoughts. Search me, O God, and know my feelings. Search me, O God, and know my desires. Empower me by your Spirit to live a life of humility. May my thoughts, words, and deeds exemplify the Humble One, Christ Jesus our Lord. Amen.

18. DETACHMENT

SUSAN PORTERFIELD CURRIE

The spiritual discipline of detachment invites us to keep company with Jesus in the wilderness. Our intentional embracing of silence and solitude commences its work of humility in us, in body and mind, heart and soul. Surely it's time to return to civilization, to our 'normal' lives of busyness and productivity and achievement.

Ah, not yet—God's rich work in us in this wilderness place is only beginning. Like Jesus, who humbled himself by taking on human flesh, and then entered into the deeper humility of death itself (Philippians 2:5-8), our faithfulness to God's deepest work invites more humility still. It is the humility of detachment.

"Whoever wants to be my disciple must deny themselves and take up their cross daily and follow me," Jesus invites (Luke 9:23, NIV). Detachment is the spiritual practice of releasing our physical, emotional, and spiritual ties to whatever controls us, manipulates us, and props up our false-self-identity. It is a daily discipline (think of Jesus' regular practice of removing himself from the demands of the crowds in order to go to a quiet place, where he could prayerfully re-center himself in the right paths of his true identity and calling) as well as a seasonal one (as when Jesus began his ministry with a forty-day intensive retreat in the wilderness, where he could prayerfully discern the false and true ways of living into his true-self-identity and calling).

Detachment—dying to sin and to temptations of the false-self—is hard work. It can be painful, and it can feel dangerous. The wilderness is not a safe place. But we don't go there alone. Jesus, who himself was ministered to by angels during his wilderness encounters with the evil one, walks alongside us, his rod and his staff protecting and comforting us.

It's helpful to remember the goal of detachment. This is not an Eastern religious emptying for the sake of being empty. It is not a hair-shirt ascetic that values pain for pain's sake. It is the path of life that Jesus modeled for us, a detaching from sin and false-self identity to make room for attaching to God and true-self fullness in him. It is a dying in order to live, a Lenten and ongoing spiritual practice that prepares us for Easter Resurrection living.

Enter into the wilderness more deeply. Let the Holy Spirit reveal your inordinate attachments, and risk the death that comes in releasing them. God, in love, is here with you, ready to deepen his life in you.

"The true self is that part of myself revealed in Christ. It is the person
I was originally created to be: my gifts, strengths, passions, interests as well as
my truest capacity to love, extend compassion, and offer hospitality.
The false self is the part of myself that I have created or was created in my upbringing
that is not true to the person God meant for me to be. In many ways
our false self is more evident than our true self. In part, this is because my true self is
revealed in God's own time and usually within community."
—Laura Swan, The Forgotten Desert Mothers

"[Detachment]... means learning to ignore the things that are not important, being
able—as one prepares for desert travel—to know what to leave behind.... It means not
taking the ego too seriously, being able to watch one's compulsive needs wilt under the
discipline of inattention."
—Belden Lane, The Solace of Fierce Landscapes

MAKE ME A CAPTIVE, LORD
A HYMN BY GEORGE MATHESON, 1842-1906

Make me a captive, Lord, and then I shall be free.
Force me to render up my sword,
And I shall conqueror be.
I sink in life's alarms, when by myself I stand;
Imprison me within thine arms,
And strong shall be my hand.

My heart is weak and poor, until its master find;
It has no spring of action sure,
It varies with the wind.
It cannot freely move till thou hast wrought its chain;
Enslave it with thy matchless love,
And deathless it shall reign.

My power is faint and low, till I have learned to serve;
It lacks the needed fire to glow,
It lacks the breeze to nerve.
It cannot drive the world, until itself be driven;
Its flag can only be unfurled
When thou shalt breathe from heaven.

REFLECTION QUESTIONS

When you find yourself in a "wilderness" place, physically, emotionally, spiritually, relationally, or circumstantially, what do you cling to for security? What fears arise? What's underneath those fears? What might God be inviting you to detach from, in order to be attached to him more deeply?

Try to describe your "false self," the self you reveal to the world but that Jesus invites you to detach from, to die to, in the desert. (What shapes your identity? What do you hide behind to give you a sense of value, meaning, or purpose? Where do you find your security? What do you try to control?) Note also what your "religious false self" looks like.

What practices could you engage in that would help you to detach from those false-self patterns?

SPIRITUAL PRACTICES

After you've preached or taught or led a presentation or completed a task, abstain from seeking feedback for a whole day. (Detach from ego.)

Go a whole day without checking email or social media. (Detach from feeling important, or from being needed.)

Identify a possession that matters to you. Give it away. (Detach from possessions.)

Take a long, realistic look at yourself in the mirror. Identify how you're aging. Pray 2 Corinthians 4:16: "Though outwardly we are wasting away, yet inwardly we are being renewed day by day." (Detach from youth and health.)

For each of the above, prayerfully note how the practice of detachment *from* makes room for attachment *to*—to God, to his love for you, to your made-for-eternity true-self in Christ.

A Prayer of Illumination:
I earnestly beg of you, Gracious Lord, to remove anything that separates me from you. Enable me to treasure Christ above all earthly goods, and lead me into discovering fully my truest self. Strip me of all that is false and unpleasing to you. In the name of Christ, our Lord. Amen.

19. ATTENTIVENESS

BR. DAVID VRYHOF, SSJE

Our experience of prayer will be forever changed when we come to understand that prayer is a gift which God gives rather than an obligation or task that we are bound as Christians to carry out. God is the initiator in the relationship, constantly awakening our hearts to life and love, wooing us, prompting our concern for others, opening our eyes to the wonders of life that inspire gratitude and praise. When we understand this – that prayer is a gift that God gives – we see that the posture of prayer is a posture of receptivity, of awareness, of attentiveness to what God is offering us, moment by moment, day by day. We learn to "pray without ceasing" by watching and listening for signs of God's presence and activity, even in the very ordinary circumstances of life. God comes to us – in a conversation with a friend, in a word from Scripture, in a moment of worship, in the beauty of nature, in the wonder of human relationships – to love us and bless us, to console us and challenge us.

A working-class woman in Ireland once put it this way: "It's like when I play hide-and-seek with the wee ones," she said. "I always leave a bit of myself sticking out. If I'm behind the curtain, I make sure my shoes are sticking out. If I'm behind the tree, I leave a little of my coat showing. I want them to find me!" God is like that: invisible to the eye, but wanting us to find him. So God "sticks out" here and there – allowing us to "see" and "hear" him in a multitude of ways – every day! When I wake up in the morning, I needn't say, "Oh, how am I going to find time to pray in such a busy day?!" Rather, I can say, "I wonder how God is going to 'stick out' in my day today? Where and when and how will God come to me today? What gifts are waiting for me in this new day?" Prayer becomes the posture of attentiveness with which I live my life – constantly attuned to signs of grace coming even in the most mundane of circumstances.

It takes practice to maintain such attentiveness and awareness. We are bombarded with "noise" and information all day long, coming at us from a host of sources. Life is reduced to text messages, YouTube videos, thousands of bits of information – all of which crowd our senses and distract us from the "still, small voice" deep within us in the place where God dwells. We certainly need times of silence and solitude in which to learn to hear this voice and become more sensitive to God's presence and activity all around us.

The late Jesuit writer Anthony de Mello compared the way most of us live to a group of people riding on a bus with the shades pulled down, missing all the scenery, while arguing with each other about things that, in the end, mean little or nothing. Living with attentiveness means pulling up the shades!

"Where can I go from your Spirit? Where can I flee from your presence? If I go up to the heavens, you are there; if I make my bed in the depths, you are there. If I rise on the wings of the dawn, if I settle on the far side of the sea, even there your hand will guide me, your right hand will hold me fast."
—Psalm 139: 7-10

"Expectant people are watchful, always looking for him they expect, always ready to find him in whatever comes along; however strange it may be, they always think he might be in it. This is what awareness of the Lord is to be like and it requires diligence that taxes a man's senses and powers to the utmost, if he is to achieve it and take God evenly in all things—if he is to find God as much in one thing as in another."
—Meister Eckhart, The Treatises

"Paying attention is not a way by which we make something happen but a way to see what is already given to us."
—Leighton Ford, The Attentive Life: Discerning God's Presence in All Things

FOR THE BEAUTY OF THE EARTH
A HYMN BY FOLLIOT S. PIERPOINT, 1864

For the beauty of the earth,
For the glory of the skies;
For the love which from our birth,
Over and around us lies;
Lord of all, to thee we raise,
This our hymn of grateful praise.

For the beauty of each hour,
Of the day and of the night;
Hill and vale, and tree and flower,
Sun and moon, and stars of light;
Lord of all, to thee we raise,
This our hymn of grateful praise.

For the joy of ear and eye,
For the heart and mind's delight;
For the mystic harmony,
Linking sense to sound and sight;
Lord of all, to thee we raise,
This our hymn of grateful praise.

For the joy of human love,
Brother, sister, parent, child;
Friends on earth and friends above,
For all gentle thoughts and mild;
Lord of all, to thee we raise,
This our hymn of grateful praise.

For thy church, that evermore,
Lifteth holy hands above;
Offering up on every shore,
Her pure sacrifice of love;
Lord of all, to thee we raise,
This our hymn of grateful praise.

For thyself, best Gift Divine,
To the world so freely given;
For that great, great love of thine,
Peace on earth, and joy in heaven;
Lord of all, to thee we raise,
This our hymn of grateful praise.

REFLECTION QUESTIONS

As you watch and listen for the signs of God's activity today, what do you notice? Record these things in a journal.

How alert are you to your senses? How do you notice God's presence in taste? touch? sight? smell? hearing?

If God is present in all places and in all things, how does that transform your life of prayer?

Looking back on the day, what gifts did you receive from God? What gifts did you receive from others?

Are you living as though the present moment is the most important moment in time?

SPIRITUAL PRACTICES

Enjoy a silent meal with others. Eat slowly. Give thanks with every bite. Notice how your taste buds come alive as you attentively enjoy your meal.

Take a slow, leisurely stroll. Note all that you notice and become aware of along the path.

Commit to remaining present with a conversation after it concludes. Notice your inner longings, fears, anxieties, moments of joy, etc.

Acknowledge the presence of God in all things and in all places. As you move through your day's events (entering a meeting, making a phone call, starting a task), give thanks for God's steady and faithful presence, moment by moment.

A Prayer of Illumination:
Omnipresent One, who is All and in all, attune my ear to the whispers of your voice; open my eyes that I might see thee in all things. As I ponder your wonder in all things, focus my distracted and divided heart that I might fully gaze upon your beauty. I rejoice and give thanks for the promise of your presence, both now and forevermore. Amen.

20. THE GIFT OF SIMPLICITY: TO WILL ONE THING

BR. DAVID VRYHOF, SSJE

One of the virtues most sought after by the early Desert Fathers and Mothers (and by generations of monastics, saints, and mystics who came after them) was the virtue of "purity of heart." "Blessed are the pure in heart," Jesus said, "for they will see God" (Matthew 5:8). To obtain this promise, these holy men and women of God rid themselves of all that was superfluous in their lives – money and possessions, luxurious clothing and rich foods, the desire for popularity, success and social status – and devoted themselves wholeheartedly to prayer, study, and good works. They examined their hearts continually to weed out envy, hatred, greed, and lust, and focused all their prayer and effort on obeying Jesus' command to "strive first for the Kingdom of God and his righteousness"(Matthew 6:33). They trusted that if they did this, God would provide them with all that was needed to sustain their lives.

Søren Kierkegaard, well-known Danish philosopher and theologian, captured the essence of "purity of heart" and of Christian simplicity in the title of his book, *Purity of Heart Is to Will One Thing*. This "one thing," he said, is God and God's Kingdom. We are to seek and love God "with all our heart, and with all our soul, and with all our mind, and with all our strength" (Mark 5:30).

This call – to "purity of heart," simplicity of life, and single-minded focus on God and God's Kingdom – is much needed today. We are overwhelmed and inundated with too much of everything: too many possessions, too much food, too much stimulation, too many activities, too much work, too much information, too many choices. As a consequence, most of us live scattered, hectic lives, racing from one task to another, juggling too many commitments, always living on the surface and never really knowing ourselves or others. Nor have we the time and space to truly know God.

The simplicity we need has both an inward dimension and an outward expression. Inwardly, it seeks an integration of the self that is rooted in our identity as beloved children of God. When we know ourselves to be children of God above all else, we find the freedom to let go of the need to compete for status, success, and popularity. We can let go of jealousy, envy, and pride. Our hearts are fixed on one thing – knowing and loving and serving God. Everything else then assumes its rightful place and order in our lives. As our hearts become pure, others will notice changes in the way we speak, the way we dress, the way we work, the way we conduct ourselves. We will grow in appreciation for ordinary things, and will be content with less. Our hearts will fill with gratitude for the beauty and wonder of creation, for the gift of life, and for the loving kindness of God. We will grow in concern for the world and its peoples, and for our environment. We will be increasingly skeptical of our consumerist culture and will grow in compassion for the poor. Our lives will become simpler, more generous, more authentic.

Why not begin (again) today? Rid yourself of whatever is getting in the way. Identify what is essential and let go of what is "too much." Resolve to seek God and God's Kingdom above all else, and examine every commitment, every relationship, every possession, every task, in the light of this one focus. Discover the gift and freedom of simplicity.

"Look at the birds of the air; they neither sow nor reap nor gather into barns, and yet your heavenly Father feeds them. Are you not of more value than they?"
—Jesus (Matthew 6:26)

"It is better to have fewer wants than to have larger resources."
—St Augustine, 354-430

"In everything, love simplicity."
—St Francis de Sales, 1567-1622

SIMPLE GIFTS
A HYMN BY ELDER JOSEPH BRACKETT, JR., 1848

'Tis the gift to be simple, 'tis the gift to be free
'Tis the gift to come down where we ought to be,
And when we find ourselves in the place just right,
'Twill be in the valley of love and delight.

When true simplicity is gained,
To bow and to bend we shan't be ashamed,
To turn, turn will be our delight,
Till by turning, turning we come 'round right.

REFLECTION QUESTIONS

How is simplicity reflected in your speech? Ask yourself, "Is what I am about to say truthful? sincere? necessary? helpful? kind?"

Review your calendar. Ask yourself, "Does my calendar reflect my values and priorities?"

How pure is your heart? How pure is your life? What is getting in the way? What doesn't belong? What is missing?

In what ways can simplicity guide your daily decisions in work, relationships, spending habits, and generosity to others?

SPIRITUAL PRACTICES

Consider Jesus' teaching in Matthew 6:25-34. How might the images of "the birds of the air" and "the lilies of the field" inspire you to live more simply? What would your life look like if you were to make Matthew 6:33 ("Strive first for the Kingdom of God...") your guiding principle?

Go through your clothes closet, your bookshelves, your storage spaces, your attic or basement, and identify the things you need. Give away the rest.

Consider ways to simplify your schedule of commitments and responsibilities. Free up space to enjoy the simpler things of life.

Practice gratitude. Look for beauty in ordinary things, in nature, and in people – every day!

A Prayer of Illumination:
Lord, grant me the serenity to accept the things I cannot change; the courage to change the things I can; and the wisdom to know the difference. (The Serenity Prayer)

21. DYING TO LIVE

JEREMY STEFANO

---◇---

The attorney supplied a stock opening line to introduce the wording of a last will and testament: "Being of sound mind… and knowing the uncertainty of this life…" The sentiment conveys less truth than the facts of living reveal. It might more appropriately read: "Being of sound mind… and knowing the certainty of death, we make this final Will and Testament."

Generally speaking, death is a subject considered from a distance and framed euphemistically in terms such as "life's uncertainty." Christians, however,consider death from another vantage point entirely. Dying is not an event to be put off until the end of life, but a reality to be reckoned with at the very beginning of following Jesus as his disciple. From that vantage point, dying is carried into one's daily life of faith with Christ, until we are brought through death into life eternal.

Through baptism the believer is personally identified with the death of Jesus and with his Resurrection from the dead. These are the events that afford to all who believe in Jesus the possibility of living a new life. What begins in identification with Jesus' death on the cross (baptism) continues in the Christian life by means of an ongoing dying, the death to sin. This ongoing commitment to giving up old ways of being is the death that must occur in each of us to make possible the rising to new life in Christ on a daily basis.

Since we are united with him in his death to sin, we are united with him in his Resurrection day by day. To be a Christian involves participating in that new life to such a degree that every believer, like Paul, can say: 'I live, but it is not me, for Christ is my life. He is the living that is now underway in me.'

The best preparation for my death is daily dying. If the Christian lives a daily dying, taking his or her leave from the world even while living in it, then part of the Christian's living is in effect preparation for dying. When death comes, we can be ready for it – indeed more than ready, since Jesus taught his disciples that whoever lives and believes in him will never die (John 11:26). Giving up on all the ways of the flesh and on all the enticements of the world, the believer is raised up in new life with Christ here and now, and through the accumulation of all one's dying, the disciple anticipates with joyful hope rising from life-by-faith to life eternal!

The fruit of being a Christian is to be alive with the secret life of Christ within, even while in the world. Living by the power of the Resurrection in the present time will surely destroy the fear of death, for one has already died on the inside and risen in Christ. What a gospel this is that proclaims a rising to new life, not only at the Last Day, but every day!

"Where, O death, is your victory?   Where, O death is your sting?"
—1 Corinthians 15:55

"Paul is ever near the cross in his own conflict with sin; in his bearing of sorrow, pain and humiliation when they come to him; in his bearing of the pains of others; in his increasing knowledge of what Calvary meant and means. But in all this he is discovering that the risen life of Jesus belongs to him, and with it great rejoicing."
—Michael Ramsey, The Resurrection of Christ

O JESUS, I HAVE PROMISED
A HYMN BY JOHN E. BODE, 1866

O Jesus, I have promised to serve Thee to the end;
Be Thou forever near me, my Master and my friend.
I shall not fear the battle if Thou art by my side,
Nor wander from the pathway if Thou wilt be my guide.

O let me feel Thee near me! The world is ever near;
I see the sights that dazzle, the tempting sounds I hear;
My foes are ever near me, around me and within;
But Jesus, draw Thou nearer, and shield my soul from sin.

O let me hear Thee speaking in accents clear and still,
Above the storm of passion, the murmurs of self-will.
And speak to reassure me, to hasten or control;
O speak and make me listen, thou guardian of my soul.

O Jesus, Thou hast promised to all who follow Thee
That where Thou art in glory there shall Thy servant be.
And Jesus, I have promised to serve Thee to the end;
O give me grace to follow, my Master and my friend.

REFLECTION QUESTIONS

How do you think and speak about death and dying?

When in your life have you experienced the power of Jesus' life at work in you?

In what ways can you seek and welcome the Lord's presence with you?

Whose death in your family was the first to impact you personally? How old were you at the time, and what do you recall about this experience as it shaped your view of death and dying?

How do these events affect you still? How are you encouraging others to face one's dying to live today?

SPIRITUAL PRACTICES

Reflect on circumstances in your life that have made the reality of life's fleeting nature known to you at a deeper level.

Recall your baptism and revisit what was said and done at the time. Perhaps you would like to renew your baptismal commitment in some way.

Find a way to celebrate and offer thanks to the Lord for your adoption into the family of God.

Give time to reading and meditating in Romans 6-8.

Think about heaven.

A Prayer of Illumination:
Lord Jesus, may I walk with you in faith today, trusting that in my dying to sin, I am brought back to life with you. And when you come to call me out of this body of death into life eternal, may I be found ready. In your name, Jesus, who conquered death for good. Amen.

22. WATCHING AND WAITING

PATRICIA TREWERN

A poignant and personal story…

As a young girl I loved to spend time with my grandmother. She was a humble woman of few words. She was also a wonderful cook, gardener, seamstress--and she loved to crochet. My favorite was the bread she made. One day I asked her to teach me how to make the delicious butter rolls she would often serve.

While teaching me her secrets for the mouthwatering recipe, she simply named each ingredient as she put it in the bowl. I noticed that some items were stirred, some were sifted, some were beaten, and the yeast was mixed with warm water. But her words were: "flour, eggs, margarine, sugar, salt, water, yeast." I had to pay close attention to see how much of each ingredient she added and what she was doing with it. Then as she began to knead the bread she said, "Watch my hands." I watched her hands closely as she folded, patted, and pushed the bread with her palms. Then she called me over and put my hands underneath hers to show me the correct technique to 'knead" the bread. After a few times she had me continue on my own. We then covered the bread for the waiting period so it could rise. After several hours, we punched the bread down and shaped it into rolls, covering it again for another time of waiting for the rolls to rise.

During the "waiting" phases we would just sit in the rocking chairs and watch the birds or we would walk out into the garden in order to check the vegetables. Not much conversation going on, but I felt so close to her.

It was quite a long process, and my grandmother used very few words to explain the recipe and her way of doing it. I had to watch her hands, watch her face, and watch her eyes to grasp all that she was teaching me. But I felt she was extremely "present" with me. I could see that she was watching me watch her. And she knew I was learning what she wanted me to know.

We baked the rolls with that smell of fresh bread wafting through the entire house. That night at dinner we had a big grin for each other as we had the first taste of our afternoon labors. When my grandfather complimented my grandmother on the delicious taste, she said with an even bigger grin, "Trish made these."

Today I think Christ speaks to us in very much the same way that my grandmother did. We listen constantly for his words. But much of the time he is wanting us to watch his hands, to focus on his ways, to keep our eyes on his. It's not that he is not answering our requests or our desire to hear from him. He is just so extremely "present" with us that words are not always the best way of communicating his message to us.

A profound spiritual lesson…

While we must take time to listen to our Lord, we must also watch him at work and wait upon him to lead, guide, and sustain. Let's not be in such a hurry to get away from his presence and be distracted by the myriad items on our "to do" list. Sit in a rocking chair, take a walk in the garden. Listen while you watch and wait. Intimacy with Christ comes during the most special, sacred, and daily times of being with him. Not always talking but listening with our ears, our heart, and our eyes. Listening with all of our senses while we watch and wait. What a joyous and refreshing time to simply live with our Lord!

"Fixing our eyes on Jesus, the pioneer and perfecter of faith."
—Hebrews 12:2

"God never hurries. There are no deadlines against which he must work.
Only to know this is to quiet our spirits and relax our nerves."
—A.W. Tozer, The Pursuit of God

IN THE GARDEN
A HYMN BY AUSTIN MILES (d. 1913)

I come to the garden alone
while the dew is still on the roses,
and the voice I hear falling on my ear
the Son of God discloses.

Refrain:
And he walks with me, and he talks with me,
and he tells me I am his own;
and the joy we share as we tarry there
none other has ever known.

He speaks, and the sound of his voice
is so sweet the birds hush their singing,
and the melody that he gave to me
within my heart is ringing.

I'd stay in the garden with him
though the night around me be falling,
but he bids me go; thru the voice of woe
his voice to me is calling.

REFLECTION QUESTIONS

Do you watch for God in the mundane activities of everyday life? In what ways does God interject himself into your daily activities, sometimes even surprising you with his grace?

When you want to hear from God, how do you prepare yourself to receive his answer? Do you always go to the same place to have communion with God?

Think of specific instances when you knew God was speaking to your spirit. How did you "hear" him? Which senses did he use to communicate with you?

How do you sense the presence of the Holy Spirit?

SPIRITUAL PRACTICES

Try choosing a different and new place to have your time alone with God. Watch the surroundings with questioning heart and a spirit of expectation.

Take a few minutes to close your eyes as you sit in God's presence. Then as you open your eyes notice everything around you. Is God speaking to you through any of your surroundings?

When something unusual or different happens in your day, take time to write down any thoughts God might be sharing with you through that experience. Then looking back through your writings and notice any repeating thoughts or recurring themes.

A Prayer of Illumination:
Teach me to listen, Holy Spirit, for your voice — in busyness and in boredom, in certainty and doubt, in noise and in silence. Teach me, Lord, to listen. Amen. —John Veltri, S.J.

23. HOLY RESTRAINT

SUSAN PORTERFIELD CURRIE

———◇———

Live life to the full! We hear this message everywhere in our culture, and we're exhorted by advertisements and slogans, teachers and coaches, go for it! We admire those who embrace the journey with a spirit of adventure, who live with boldness and gusto and passion. Why, even Jesus said, "I have come that they may have life, and have it to the full" (John 10:10)!

And then we come into a season of release. We don't mean a season or experience that's imposed on us (an experience of darkness, or withholding, of diminishing returns; a season, in contrast to life, of death)—we may attribute that to the havoc of sin in the world, or perhaps to the pruning work of a sovereign God. No, we mean a season that we enter willingly, even intentionally, as active participants in the spiritual dynamic at work when we do so.

What otherwise would feel like a constraint becomes restraint—holy restraint. As a spiritual practice, it's something we engage in not for its own sake, as if it's somehow more holy in and of itself to restrain. The apostle Paul, when writing of eating or not eating food sacrificed to idols (1 Corinthians 10), notes that neither eating nor refraining from eating has merit in and of itself. What makes an action holy is the intent behind it and the engagement with God in it.

Holy restraint (more precisely, holy self-restraint, since it's something we put on ourselves rather than on others) is a deliberate holding back—of our words, our effort—for the sake of leaving more room in which to notice God. It is not a disengagement of the heart or soul or mind, as if we stop caring about who or what we're present to. When done well, and in humility, it allows for others to engage for themselves directly with God's heart. And it humbles our own gifts (be they words of wisdom, acts of strength, etc.), so that we grow in trusting God, that what he has brought to our attention is something he is already doing in or for us and in or for the other(s), and that he will reveal it to us or to them directly in his own time.

Jesus practices holy restraint. When the woman caught in adultery is brought before him, instead of preaching a sermon or seizing the teaching opportunity, he quietly breaks eye contact and scribbles in the sand at the crowd's feet. The consequence? Instead of hiding behind personally safe theological debate or judiciary argumentation, those who are gathered each hear the inner conviction of the Holy Spirit. Several months later, when Jesus himself is on trial, he speaks very little and does less, restraining himself not only in word but in powerful action. Certainly, there are occasions when he does speak, and preach, and heal, and command the wind and the waves with a shout. But he knows when to unleash, and when to restrain, and both are in the Spirit, and thus holy.

As we journey the way of holy restraint in our personal lives, let us travel trustingly with Jesus to the holy restraint of the Cross—and find there fullness of life indeed!

Philippians 2:5-11 invites us to identify with Jesus in this practice of holy restraint—Jesus, whose word and power created the universe, and who, through his humble self-restraint, is exalted above all.

*"In your relationships with one another, have the same mindset as
Christ Jesus: Who, being in very nature God, did not consider equality
with God something to be used to his own advantage; rather, he made himself
nothing.... to the glory of God the Father."*
—Philippians 2: 5-7, 11

*"Oh, brothers and sisters, let us beware! Unless we make
the increase of humility our study, we may find that we have been
delighting in beautiful thoughts and feelings, in solemn acts of consecration
and faith, while the only sure mark of the presence of God—the disappearance
of self—was missing the entire time. Come and let us flee to Jesus, and hide ourselves
in Him until we are clothed with His humility. That alone is our holiness."*
—Andrew Murray, Humility and Sin, page 72.

AT THE NAME OF JESUS
LYRICS BY CAROLINE MARIA NOEL, 1890

At the name of Jesus, Every knee shall bow,
Every tongue confess Him King of glory now;
'Tis the Father's pleasure We should call Him Lord,
Who from the beginning Was the mighty Word.

Humbled for a season, To receive a name
From the lips of sinners, Unto whom He came,
Faithfully He bore it Spotless to the last,
Brought it back victorious, When from death He passed.

Bore it up triumphant, With its human light,
Through all ranks of creatures, To the central height,
To the throne of Godhead, To the Father's breast;
Filled it with the glory Of that perfect rest.

Christians, this Lord Jesus Shall return again,
With His Father's glory O'er the earth to reign;
For all wreaths of empire Meet upon His brow,
And our hearts confess Him King of glory now.

REFLECTION QUESTIONS

When you voluntarily refrain from offering words of wisdom, counsel, or exhortation, or from having the last word no matter how godly it is, what goes on in you? What do you notice that might invite a dying-to of something false/sinful in you? What do you have to trust God with?

Besides restraining from words, what else do you tend to offer to others that might become an opportunity for practicing holy restraint? (Something that's about your gifts, your calling, the way in which you tend to interact that might evoke pridefulness?) In this holy restraint, what goes on between you and God?

In what ways can you embrace holy restraint on an ongoing basis?

SPIRITUAL PRACTICES

When praying with others, try expressing your prayer simply by saying "Lord, I hold — (the concern) — before you," and refrain from using more words. What do you notice?

Try eating a communal meal in silence. What goes on in you that's about you? What goes on in you that's about the others? What goes on in you that's about your awareness of God's presence? What about the awkwardness you might be experiencing?

Identify a practice that you tend to do with an extravagance of energy (post on social media sites? grocery shop? exercise?). Try doing it with restraint. What do you notice about yourself? about God?

A Prayer of Illumination:
Lord Jesus Christ, who humbled yourself even unto death so that we would be given fullness of life by your Spirit and in your Father's love, grant us humility in word and deed; that in the discipline of holy restraint we, and those whom we companion, would better hear your voice, and see your ways, to the glory of your name. Amen.

24. SELF-KNOWLEDGE

TED WUESTE

In his great theological work *The Institutes of the Christian Religion*, John Calvin made the observation that "Nearly all the wisdom we possess, that is to say true and sound wisdom, consists of two parts: the knowledge of God and of ourselves." Socrates famously commented that "the unexamined life is not worth living."

While the wisdom of the ages seems to agree that self-knowledge is vital, contemporary culture and practice often lead us in a different direction. First, self-knowledge requires slowing down enough to take an inward look and becoming quiet enough to listen. Our technologically advanced modern world affords neither, in the natural flow of life. With screens always in front of us and noises always around us, we have a constant encouragement to stay focused outward. Second, we do not have many people teaching us practices that can help us develop self-knowledge in ways that are reliable for our spiritual journey. Finally, many well-meaning followers of Jesus misunderstand the call to self-knowledge and subsequently dismiss introspection as self-indulgence or self-preoccupation (resulting in self-ignorance).

The challenge to self-knowledge is one that can certainly go awry if not directed toward the proper end, but it is grounded in the idea that we can apply the realities of the gospel only to the actual conditions of our hearts. If we are ignorant of inner motives and desires, we are not able to surrender ourselves fully. If we are not aware of specific insecurities or fears, how are we able to rely upon God's love and presence in our lives? Because God is relational, we must relate to Him in the truth of our hearts, making all of who we are available to him. If we stay "in our heads," then God's love becomes a pleasant abstraction or simply sweet words and not the transforming force that we believe the gospel to be.

In Luke 9:23, Jesus teaches, "If any would come after me, let him deny himself." The word *deny* means to refuse, and one needs to know oneself in order to refuse oneself. Deny does not mean to ignore or forget or dismiss but to refuse in favor of Jesus' heart and desires. When we simply ignore or forget self, the powerful motives of our hidden hearts can wreak havoc on our attempts to follow Jesus. When we bring inner realities to the light through self-knowledge, we are able to deny them joyfully, even if painfully, in order to listen to his voice.

Two primary fears can also hinder our attempts at healthy self-knowledge. First, we can worry that there is too much underneath the surface that is ugly, and the voice of shame can arise. Second, we can become paralyzed by the task, concerned that we will not be able to see all that is there. Beautifully and predictably, our gracious God meets us in these fears as he reminds us in his Word that he searches our hearts and leads us where we need to go (Psalm 139:23-24). Certainly, there is a tendency for our hearts to be mired in deceit and shame, but he promises to search and heal and save when we open ourselves to him (Jeremiah 17:9-10, 14) and join him in searching our hearts.

"Being filled yet unfulfilled comes from being without deep interiority.
When there is never time or space to stand behind our own lives and
look reflectively at them, then the pressures and distractions of life
simply consume us, until we lose control over our lives."
—Ronald Rolheiser, The Shattered Lantern

CLEANSE ME
A HYMN BY J. EDWIN ORR

Search me, O God,
and know my heart today,
Try me, O Savior,
know my thoughts, I pray;
See if there be some wicked way in me;
Cleanse me from every sin and set me free.

I praise Thee, Lord,
for cleansing me from sin;
Fulfill Thy word and make me pure within;
Fill me with fire,
where once I burned with shame;
Grant my desire to magnify Thy name.

Lord, take my life,
and make it wholly Thine;
Fill my poor heart with
Thy great love divine;
Take all my will, my passion, self and pride;
I now surrender, Lord, in me abide.

REFLECTION QUESTIONS

What do you desire? To what degree are your desires shaped by a false sense of self versus your true "in Christ" self?

How aware are you of specific sins in your life? Are there places of woundedness in your life that you have ignored?

How often do you turn off all your technology? What would it be like to be "off the grid" for even a short time? What might this afford your soul?

Do you have others in your life who are able and willing to act as a mirror for you to grow in self-knowledge? How often to do you simply ask the Lord to search your heart?

SPIRITUAL PRACTICES

Simply pray "Search me, O God, and know my heart" (Ps 139:23) and wait quietly for your gracious Father to disclose his heart and your heart to you.

Open your heart and life to others (a trusted friend, a counselor, a spiritual director) and prayerfully listen to God's wisdom through another … James 5:16, "Confess your sins to each other and pray for each other so that you may be healed."

Journal your thoughts, desires, hopes, and prayers. Ask the Lord to give insight into the contents of your heart.

Sit with the Psalms and notice what seems to connect with your heart. (Hebrews 4:12)

A Prayer of Illumination:
Father, I praise You for knowing and loving all of me. I know that You see more beauty in me that I can imagine and You also hold the dark parts of me with grace. I entrust myself to You to show me what I need to see when I need to see it. May I never shy away from embracing the truth of me, so that I can live ever closer to Your heart and therefore reflect Your glory. Amen.

25. CONTENTMENT

ANGELA WISDOM

♦

We live in a world in which things are not as they ought to be. We long for more; we long for peace, serenity, health, justice, and prosperity. Like a storm on a raging sea, our souls, our communities, and the world all churn with discontentment. Yet Christian contentment is a gift of God to every believer who seeks first his kingdom and his righteousness (Matthew 6). It is a reality for the believer in the darkest, most turbulent of circumstances and conditions.

The 17th-century Puritan pastor Jeremiah Burroughs encourages believers to embrace this "rare jewel" in "sad and sinking times." He defines Christian contentment as "that sweet, inward, quiet, gracious frame of spirit, which freely submits to and delights in God's wise and fatherly disposal in every condition." We can rest in the assurance that even when we feel deprived or insecure, there is a greater good at work that we may not see. We can humbly submit to and trust in God's providence.

Maturing in discernment is critical to the believer's growth in holy contentment. Without it, we may become complacent when life is easy. Perhaps we find our senses dulled to God's heart for justice in a broken world and judge others who are rightly moved by a particular injustice. Or perhaps we are discontent in circumstances that God intends for our good. In times of restlessness or insecurity, we may be tempted to amass experiences, possessions, relationships, or opportunities in an effort to feel valued or secure. When we are either complacent or discontent, the net result can be the same: we become unwilling to take uncomfortable, risky steps of faith in the direction God wants to lead us. Remember how the Israelites grumbled while in the wilderness, lacking trust that God would be faithful to bring them to the land of milk and honey as he had promised?

For the Christian, this should not be so. As we mature in faith, grow in discernment, and allow God to develop our spiritual senses to be responsive to his Spirit, we can live a life of true contentment. As Paul says, "Since we walk by the Spirit, let us keep in step with the Spirit" (Galatians 5:25). In uncertain times, the believer is moved to prayer, seeking God for his perspective, that he may quiet our unsettled spirits with his love and restore our hope in him (Zephaniah 3:17). God's economy is generous to all and provides all we need. We can trust him in all circumstances and delight even in difficult conditions, knowing that he is faithful. In turn, trusting God stirs us to action as he calls us to participate in his mission to change our hearts, revitalize our communities, and bring peace to the world.

Jesus said that the Kingdom of God is a treasure worth selling everything to attain (Matthew 13). May we treasure this priceless pearl, content knowing that when we belong to Christ, we lack no good thing.

"Oh, taste and see that the Lord is good! Blessed is the man who takes refuge in him! Oh, fear the Lord, you his saints, for those who fear him have no lack! The young lions suffer want and hunger; but those who seek the Lord lack no good thing."
—Psalm 34:8-10 (ESV)

"To be well skilled in the mystery of Christian contentment is the duty, glory and excellence of a Christian."
—Jeremiah Burroughs

ETERNAL FATHER, STRONG TO SAVE
A HYMN BY WILLIAM WHITING, 1860

Eternal Father, strong to save,
Whose arm hath bound the restless wave,
Who bidd'st the mighty ocean deep
Its own appointed limits keep;
Oh, hear us when we cry to Thee,
For those in peril on the sea!

O Christ! Whose voice the waters heard
And hushed their raging at Thy word,
Who walkedst on the foaming deep,
And calm amidst its rage didst sleep;
Oh, hear us when we cry to Thee,
For those in peril on the sea!

Most Holy Spirit! Who didst brood
Upon the chaos dark and rude,
And bid its angry tumult cease,
And give, for wild confusion, peace;
Oh, hear us when we cry to Thee,
For those in peril on the sea!

O Trinity of love and power!
Our brethren shield in danger's hour,
From rock and tempest, fire and foe,
Protect them wheresoe'er they go;
Thus evermore shall rise to Thee
Glad hymns of praise from land and sea.

REFLECTION QUESTIONS

How does God quiet you with his love when you are discontent?

To what degree have you experienced a sense of being freely submitted to and delighting in God's wise and fatherly disposal in every condition?

What are some ways you sense you have freely joined God in his mission in your heart, in your community, in the world? Are there ways you have resisted him?

Is there a person or community of people you know who seem discontent? Has there been an issue of injustice that has stirred this reaction?

SPIRITUAL PRACTICES

Meditate on Hebrews 13:5-6 or Philippians 4:11-12 and confess any sin of discontentment present in your soul due to dissatisfaction with what God has given you. Receive his forgiveness.

Live simply and contentedly, delighting in what you have been given.

Allow yourself to be stirred to action on behalf of others when God gives you his perspective on an issue of injustice or oppression in the world.

Pray for God to give you his heart for yourself, your community, and your world.

A Prayer of Illumination:
In sad and sinking times, Lord, may we treasure the rare jewel of Christian contentment available to us in your kingdom on earth and in heaven for your glory. Amen.

26. EMBRACING MYSTERY

TED WUESTE

In Romans 11:33, we find a sublime description of God and his ways: "Oh, the depths of the riches and wisdom and knowledge of God! How unsearchable are his judgments and how inscrutable his ways!" While there is so much we know with clarity, there is much about who God is, Father, Son and Holy Spirit, and how he works in the world, that is mysterious and hidden from our sight. It is beyond us.

The unknown might be palatable to us when it comes to how he created the world or how the stars hang in place, but we can experience significant angst regarding the ways that he is or isn't at work in our personal lives. Part of finite humanity's interaction with an infinite God requires that we live with a sense of mystery. In addition, it appears that God's wisdom leads him to reveal some things to us and withhold other things. Mystery and the unknown are realities of the human condition.

However, rather than being a nuisance, living in the unknown is the beauty of the human-divine relationship. Embracing mystery leads us into trust and dependence which is our created design! Bill Volkman, in his book on contemplative prayer, suggests, "Like Adam and Eve, we all have been given the same basic commandment: 'From any tree of the garden you may eat freely; but from the tree of the knowledge of good and evil you shall not eat.' But, like Adam and Eve, most of us continue to make the mistake of choosing to eat of the fruit of the tree of knowledge, or the tree of knowing, instead of in faith taking from the Tree of Life, the Tree of Unknowing."

This is why the German poet Rainer Maria Rilke wrote, "Have patience with everything that remains unsolved in your heart. Try to love the questions themselves, like locked rooms and like books written in a foreign language." The encouragement to love the questions flows from the realities of what God does in us through the unknown and invisible purposes of the Triune God. He allows us to be in places--and even pushes us into places--where it is very clear we are not in control.

Here's the amazing, freeing, humbling reality: God is so much bigger and more complex and exciting and mind-bending than we could ever imagine. Doesn't it stand to reason, then, that mystery has to be a part of the journey? It is a good thing when it leads us to deepening dependence.

So, how do we embrace mystery and the unknown? First, pray honestly and give God your frustrations and fears. Second, with his help, reframe your experience of mystery from being a loss to being a gain. Third, let go of the need to know, and rest in the joy of trusting that you do not truly need to know ... at least for now.

"Above all else, trust the slow work of God. We are quite naturally impatient in everything to reach the end without delay. We should like to skip the intermediate stages. We are impatient of being on the way to something unknown, something new. Only God could say what this new spirit gradually forming in you will be. Give our Lord the benefit that His hand is leading you, and accept the anxiety of feeling yourself in suspense, and incomplete."
—Pierre Teilhard de Chardin

GOD MOVES IN A MYSTERIOUS WAY
A HYMN BY WILLIAM COWPER, 1774

God moves in a mysterious way
His wonders to perform;
He plants His footsteps in the sea
And rides upon the storm.
Deep in unfathomable mines
Of never failing skill
He treasures up His bright designs
And works His sov'reign will.

Ye fearful saints, fresh courage take;
The clouds ye so much dread
Are big with mercy and shall break
In blessings on your head.
Judge not the Lord by feeble sense,
But trust Him for His grace;
Behind a frowning providence
He hides a smiling face.

His purposes will ripen fast,
Unfolding every hour;
The bud may have a bitter taste,
But sweet will be the flow'r.
Blind unbelief is sure to err
And scan His work in vain;
God is His own interpreter,
And He will make it plain.

REFLECTION QUESTIONS

In what areas of life are uncertainty and mystery the most difficult for you? Relationships? Career? Finances? Future plans?

In what ways are you tempted to gain certainty when you are in a place of unknowing? Denial? Deceit? Dominance?

What questions and places of unknowing are present in your life?

How might God be using mystery to produce deeper trust in you?

SPIRITUAL PRACTICES

Prayerfully journal current places of uncertainty in your life as well as your response to them.

Ask God to lead your heart and mind in an imaginative exercise. First, consider the way(s) in which a place of uncertainty could be a joy rather than a burden. Second, imagine new responses based on joy rather than fear.

Reflect on the emotions that mystery and the unknown elicit in you. How might your emotional responses lead you away from trust?

Engage in meditative prayer. Set aside 10-20 minutes to simply sit in quietness of heart with the Lord. Prayerfully, choose a prayer word that expresses your trust in God. As issues of unknowing or other thoughts arise, simply let the thoughts go and return to meditating on your prayer word.

A Prayer of Illumination:
Father, I worship you as the one who knows all things and holds all things in your holy, gracious hands. I admit that I often want to know things more than I want to trust your timing and your ways. Give me the courage to let go of the tree of knowing and rest in unknowing. I desire to trust you more than I want to know. In the name of Jesus, Amen.

27. SEASONS OF THE SOUL

DIANA CURREN BENNETT

———◇———

The word *season* has many nuances: time of year, situation in life, stage of spiritual development, or perhaps spiritual health. A season represents a fairly well-defined period of time in our lives, whether it is physical or spiritual. It is important to recognize that there are "seasons of the soul" that require our attention, understanding, and care.

Identifying the different seasons in light of how well we know God and ourselves can become a significant tool in trusting God. In considering the seasons, it helps to visualize the more common understanding of the seasons of the year: winter, spring, summer, and fall.

Winter is a time of dormancy in anticipation of a new awakening. As with the other seasons, winter has its positive and negative nuances. Winter can be a delightful season, resting from the rigors of fall. The ground is resting, and so are we. If we are in a bleak winter spiritually, God seems far away. We might feel despondent or unproductive. It might be a time of the dark night of the soul.

Spring can be a messy season, filled with sudden warmth and dreary days. Days of clouds and rain alternate with dry, sunny ones. Buds and blossoms appear. Spiritually, spring is a time when our love for God is stirring anew and we feel alive. We are excited about new opportunities and are ready to consider undertaking new commitments to ourselves and to others.

Summer is the season for cultivating. We begin to see the fruit of our labors, as well as those things that "didn't take." We may have tackled many new projects in the spring and now need to step back and reevaluate what stays and what needs to be uprooted. Summer can also be a time of needed rest for the body and soul.

Fall, ideally, is the season of harvesting fruit. We hope it will be a season of thanksgiving as we savor the faithfulness of God and the satisfaction of work done well in his strength. There's no doubt, however, that fall can be a discouraging season if we are looking for fruit and find a poor crop instead.

Our own spiritual experience often meanders in and out of the seasons. The Christian spiritual journey involves starting and stopping, digressions and sometimes reversion to a previous season. We may be experiencing a winter season even though the calendar says summer, or experiencing fall when it is springtime outside.

Reflecting on our current season can be a litmus test for prayer, yearning, action . . . and even resting and trusting God with it all. The seasons become lenses for viewing our spiritual health and considering what particular spiritual practice might move us closer to Christ-likeness. By God's grace, we move toward that goal. Whatever season you find yourself in spiritually, fully inhabit it without rushing into the next season. God has something for us to "be present to" in every season. Trust that he is always at work in you with divine purpose.

"There is a time for everything, and a season for every activity under the heavens."
—Ecclesiastes 3:1

*"I would not consider any spirituality worthwhile that wants to walk in sweetness
and ease and run from the imitation of Christ."*
—John of the Cross

IN THE CROSS OF CHRIST I GLORY
A HYMN BY JOHN BOWRING, 1825

In the cross of Christ I glory,
Towering o'er the wrecks of time;
All the light of sacred story
Gathers round its head sublime.

When the woes of life o'ertake me,
Hopes deceive and fears annoy,
Never shall the cross forsake me;
Lo! It glows with peace and joy.

When the sun of bliss is beaming
Light and love upon my way,
From the cross the radiance streaming
Adds more luster to the day.

Bain and blessing, pain and pleasure
By the cross are sanctified,
Peace is there that knows no measure;
Joys that thru all time abide.

REFLECTION QUESTIONS

As you consider the state and season of your soul, do you sense neglect? If so, what comes to mind as a particular symptom? For example, you may be discouraged, busy, yet bored, or wanting to withdraw from responsibility and leadership. Identify your soul season.

When have you felt most spiritually alive? What was happening in your life at that time? Were there any spiritual practices that were energizing to you? What season best describes this situation?

When have you felt the least spiritually alive? Reflect on possible causes. What season of the soul defines times when your soul is less alive than usual?

In your most difficult seasons, who in your life or what activity brings you the most comfort?

SPIRITUAL PRACTICES

The journal is the sketchbook of the soul. If you have recorded highs and lows over time, revisit your journal and notice the presence of God during these times. Reviewing journal entries and outcomes creates a deeper sense of trust regardless of the season.

If you do not keep a journal, consider beginning the practice. This is not a practice of recording what you did and when, but a time to reflect and record the season and the responses of your soul. The journal is a place to record moods, personal disciplines or lack thereof, temptations, failures, answered prayers and celebrations.

Consider daily Examen prayer. Quietly reflect on what gives you life or what is life-draining. Present these situations to God. Pray and listen to God's voice for direction, whether in a season of desolation or consolation.

A Prayer of Illumination:
Loving God, we are grateful for your presence in our lives, the empowerment of the Holy Spirit, and the knowledge that you care and are in control of our lives. Help us to trust you not only in those productive seasons where we constantly feel your presence, but also in those dry and dark seasons when we are uncertain. Help us to be steadfast at all times. Amen.

COMPANIONSHIP

28. SPIRITUAL FRIENDSHIP

RICK ANDERSON

◇

A friend is a gift, but a spiritual friend is a sacred gift. A spiritual friend is someone who not only challenges you in your spiritual journey but also treats you just as Jesus would in your fallen state: grace before truth, friendship over formula. A spiritual friend is someone you know very well, but more importantly, someoneyou've allowed to know you. You've granted them access to your inner life of joy and despair, desire and fear, giftedness and struggle, competence and insecurity.

God, in his providence, has seen fit to give us the opportunity to both bless and wound one another. Many of us carry wounds from the words or deeds of a fellow mortal that pierced deeply. For some of us, these wounds accompany us like a shadow. There is something of a mystery in the way the Immortal God often sends healing through yet another fellow mortal, speaking God's healing sentiments as a balm for the wounded soul. It is one thing to cognitively know "I am dearly loved" and another thing to see, hear, and feel it. Spiritual friends have the ability to make God's love experiential.

In life's journey together, the encouragement of a spiritual friend in both word and embrace become incarnational. In this way, we are the arms and voice of God to one another. It's true. If we believe that God's voice can be delivered through the pastor in the pulpit, or that his tangible creativity can be touched and observed in the natural world, is it such a stretch to think his words and affection could inhabit a sacred companion who is available to the Spirit's nudge? That incarnational quality is why this friendship can be described as a sacred gift. A friend like this understands the honor and stewardship of being used by God in such powerful ways and is receptive to having their own soul touched by those God would send as his message bearers.

A spiritual friend has the ability to challenge and spur on, based upon their first-hand knowledge of the tremendous potential God has placed in you. This friend can lovingly challenge you in areas where your attitudes and behaviors seem at odds with God's desires. This friend has the opportunity to pour courage into you about living into your true self. "I see something in you that is unique and God-graced," they say. "I want to affirm it and see more of that released." They affirm that which is already in play and call out that which insecurely remains on the sidelines. God must smile when this happens.

Are you blessed to have even one friend like this? If so, you are very fortunate. If not, you are certainly not alone in your desire for a companion like this! Sometimes the best way to begin is to take steps toward offering this type of friendship to others and see who responds. Be the arms and voice of God to others today! And may you incarnate the love of God in fresh ways through the gift of spiritual friendship.

"Most of us have friends. We have friends who are interested in the same things we are interested in. We have friends who share our faith perspectives. We have friends who help us. But in my mind, the best kind of friends are 'soul friends.' These are people with whom I can be forthcoming and honest about my own soul. In return, they reflect God's love for me in their words, their attitudes and their actions. These are friends who 'enflesh' God for me. God loves and nourishes my soul through these friends."
—Alice Fryling, Seeking God Together

"If you are blessed to have one or more genuine spiritual friendships, be sure to thank God, because such friendships are not an entitlement but a gift ... Spiritual friendship is not a reward for good behavior. It is the means by which God reveals his goodness by helping us know others and ourselves and thereby know him. It is a gift God gives to us. It is a gift we can give to others."
—David Benner, Sacred Companions

WHAT A FRIEND WE HAVE IN JESUS
A HYMN BY JOSEPH M. SCRIVEN, 1955

What a friend we have in Jesus,
All our sins and griefs to bear!
What a privilege to carry
Everything to God in prayer!
O what peace we often forfeit,
O what needless pain we bear,
All because we do not carry
Everything to God in prayer.

Have we trials and temptations?
Is there trouble anywhere?
We should never be discouraged;
Take it to the Lord in prayer.
Can we find a friend so faithful,
Who will all our sorrows share?
Jesus knows our every weakness;
Take it to the Lord in prayer.

Are we weak and heavy laden,
Cumbered with a load of care?
Precious Savior, still our refuge;
Take it to the Lord in prayer.

REFLECTION QUESTIONS

In a time of prayerful reflection, ask, "How well am I listening/attending in my friend-ships?"

What can I see, affirm, and call forth that my friend may not know about himself/herself?

In what ways can I be the "arms and voice of God" to those in my reach today?

Is there a sin I should confess to a brother/sister?

SPIRITUAL PRACTICES

List the names of one or two spiritual friends in your life.

Inquire of the Lord as to how he might lead you to greater honesty and/or vulnerability in these friendships.

Spend time thanking God for these friendships.

Ask God to reveal ways to deepen your bonds of trust, affection, and loyalty.

A Prayer of Illumination:
Loving Father, you are faithful and good in all things. Thank you for calling me your friend through the reconciliation that I now have in Christ Jesus. My heart is filled with gratitude that Christ is the dearest and the most trusted friend I could ever know. There is none other as faithful, loving, caring, and precious as he. Teach me Lord, by your Spirit, to be a spiritual companion to those whom you're drawing me toward. And thank you for the sacred friendships that you've used to enrich my life. All praise, honor, and glory be to you, gracious God! Amen.

29. SPIRITUAL DIRECTION

JEREMY STEFANO

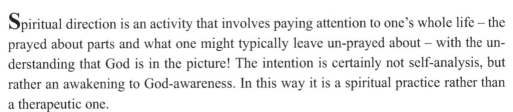

Spiritual direction is an activity that involves paying attention to one's whole life – the prayed about parts and what one might typically leave un-prayed about – with the understanding that God is in the picture! The intention is certainly not self-analysis, but rather an awakening to God-awareness. In this way it is a spiritual practice rather than a therapeutic one.

The focus is not on what one *should* believe or know about God, but on what one actually is experiencing. The raw material for prayerful reflection is one's being and doing, one's actual praying and living. Getting beneath the surface of all the comings and goings, to the hidden sources that inform and direct one's ways, is the intent. When done consistently, spiritual direction will encourage an ever-deepening awareness of the distinctive but oft-overlooked presence, initiative, and activity of the Holy Spirit, while sharpening discernment regarding how one may or may not be "in step with the Spirit."

In myriad ways the Lord calls his people to the awareness of his persistent presence and leading. These include personal reading of Scripture, hearing the Word preached, the Lord's promptings in the heart, words spoken by friends, and so on. Spiritual direction is simply another such means, and a valuable one in that it has the potential to bring light to experiences that ordinarily would pass unnoticed. Like much of what the Spirit does, it is unpretentious, in that spiritual direction takes place amidst the simplicity of dialog between two people. To guard against the encounter's devolving into mere chatter, and to attend to what the Spirit is doing or saying, requires intentionality. The result is a prayerful conversation that can blend rest with intensity, reverence with humor, grief with hope, all with unforced authenticity.

A defining hallmark is the quality of listening involved. It is really the gift of listening that transforms the ordinary conversation into an extra-ordinary experience of being found before God. The one who listens is not merely taking in the story, but watching and waiting on God with the person--and sometimes *for* the person--who is doing the sharing. The listener is not looking to find a solution to a presenting problem or an answer to a pressing question. The listener is, well, listening. And in so doing, the person will be prayerfully accompanied to a discovery of their own. Sometimes the listener is the one who discerns the Spirit's direction or presence. Either way, God is heeded and attended to with faith.

Many things are required in a listener for this kind of conversation. Prayerfulness is primary. Humility, grace, and subtlety allow the listener to be unobtrusive and remain of secondary importance to the person's encounter with God. In the spiritual direction relationship, it is understood that the listener is there entirely for the sake of the seeker.

"Jesus turned and saw them following him. He asked them, 'What are you looking for?'" (John 1:38)

"The premise [of spiritual direction] is that God is always at work in us, continually directing our lives through his Holy Spirit so that we are being shaped into the image of Christ, and by noticing that presence of God at work in us, we can more fully respond to, cooperate with, and grow in graced communion with the Triune God."
—Susan Porterfield Currie, Director, Selah Certificate Program in Spiritual Direction, Leadership Transformations, Inc.

HOLY SPIRIT, TRUTH DIVINE
A HYMN BY SAMUEL LONGFELLOW, 1864

Holy Spirit, Truth divine,
Dawn upon this soul of mine;
Word of God and inward light
Wake my spirit, clear my sight.

Holy Spirit, Love divine,
Glow within this heart of mine;
Kindle every high desire;
Perish self in Thy pure fire.

Holy Spirit, Power divine,
Fill and nerve this will of mine;
Be my Lord and I shall be
Firmly bound, forever free.

Holy Spirit, Joy divine,
Gladden Thou this heart of mine;
In the desert ways I sing,
"Spring, O Well, forever spring."

REFLECTION QUESTIONS

"What are you looking for?"

Do you ever find yourself or others explaining what God is doing or intending when bad things happen?

How are your beliefs about God different from your experience of God?
Do you find freedom in rejoicing with those who rejoice and grieving with those who mourn?

Who in your life is present to the deeper things – or, perhaps, who is attentive to the ordinary things in your life in a deeper way? While a formal relationship with a spiritual director may be desirable, it may not always be possible.

SPIRITUAL PRACTICES

Ask God to show you his interest in parts of your life that do not seem important or that feel like a waste of time.

Be attentive to what God is doing in others.

When in conversation with a friend, practice restraint by considering whether or not to offer an opinion before you speak.

Be patient with yourself and others.

Consider receiving spiritual direction. Finding the right spiritual director may take time, so ask the Lord to lead you to the right person.

A Prayer of Illumination:
Breathe on me, Breath of God, fill me with life anew, that I may love what Thou dost love, and do what Thou wouldst do. Amen. (Edwin Hatch. 1835-1889)

30. HOSPITALITY

JOELLEN MAURER

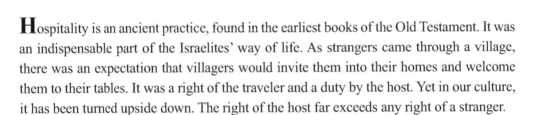

Hospitality is an ancient practice, found in the earliest books of the Old Testament. It was an indispensable part of the Israelites' way of life. As strangers came through a village, there was an expectation that villagers would invite them into their homes and welcome them to their tables. It was a right of the traveler and a duty by the host. Yet in our culture, it has been turned upside down. The right of the host far exceeds any right of a stranger.

Our culture thinks that to be hospitable to another we must have a perfect table set, gourmet food served, 800-count bed sheets, and pima cotton towels. Yes, hospitality can happen in our homes and often does, but hospitality is not about entertaining well. It is about welcoming others into a place where they can be known and inviting them into a deeper relationship with you, others and Christ. And that can happen anywhere.

As newlyweds in a tiny fixer-upper home, we were challenged to open up our doors. To invite people in. To welcome them into our lives. Because if we started to do that in our tiny home, we would do it wherever we ended up. And we did. And we do. Because we learned that to be hospitable means we are fully present to others when they are with us. It means that we are willing to open up and share what we have. It means that we are generous with our lives and our things. And it means that we are intentional about living our lives in community.

One of the most dramatic scenes in the musical *Les Misérables* is when the bishop invites the stranger, Jean Valjean, into his home, feeds him, and gives him a place to sleep. Valjean sneaks out in the middle of the night with the silver from the bishop's table and, when caught, is certain he will be thrown back into prison. But the discerning bishop tells the officers that he gave Valjean the silver--and then proceeds to hand him the candlesticks as well. A word from the bishop--"I have bought your soul for God"-- is a grace extended, an invitation for Valjean to be something more than a thief. It is a transformative moment for Valjean.

We all are strangers in this world. A world that provides few places of rest and restoration, safety and spiritual renewal, a warm piece of bread and a cool cup of water. May we be the ones who will invite others to a space that is grace-filled and love-drenched. May we be the ones who will welcome the stranger and make them a friend. May we provide words of transformation and grace. And may God's welcoming heart profoundly move us to share that welcoming heart with a lost and lonely world.

"When God's people are in need, be ready to help them.
Always be eager to practice hospitality."
—Romans 12:13 NLT

"We can incarnate the welcoming heart of God for the world. God welcomes
strangers, inviting them to share his home and get to know his family."
—Adele Calhoun, Spiritual Disciplines Handbook

SOFTLY AND TENDERLY
A HYMN BY WILL L. THOMPSON, 1880

Softly and tenderly Jesus is calling,
Calling for you and for me;
See, on the portals He's waiting and watching,
Watching for you and for me.

Refrain: Come home, come home,
You who are weary, come home;
Earnestly, tenderly, Jesus is calling,
Calling, O sinner, come home!

Why should we tarry when Jesus is pleading,
Pleading for you and for me?
Why should we linger and heed not His mercies,
Mercies for you and for me?

Oh, for the wonderful love He has promised,
Promised for you and for me!
Though we have sinned, He has mercy and pardon,
Pardon for you and for me.

REFLECTION QUESTIONS

Looking back over the years, what has most held you back from practicing hospitality?

How about now? Are there things that hinder you from being welcoming and inviting?

Is there someone you feel pulled to invite and welcome into a deeper relationship? Who? How will you reach out to them this week?

What was the time and place you most felt welcomed? When have you experienced soul hospitality? What was most striking about these experiences?

What might it look like to intentionally work on noticing Christ in your midst when you are with others?

SPIRITUAL PRACTICES

Look around at the people you encounter today. Ask yourself what you might do to serve them.

Look around your church. Look for those who may not feel welcome, and invite them to join you...for anything.

Read Luke 10:38-42. Use Lectio Divina to consider Mary and Martha's hospitality prayerfully and reflectively. Notice any invitation that emerges from your prayers.

Thank someone who has shown you hospitality recently. Send them a note today to share your appreciation.

A friend once confessed that when people leave her home, she hopes they feel better about themselves than when they walked in. Welcome others in such a way that they feel better about themselves when they leave.

A Prayer of Illumination
Gracious Father, as we consider what it is you have done to invite us into your presence and make us welcome in your family, we ask that you open our eyes and ears to those who feel alone in this world. May we more deeply understand the grace you have offered us, and may we allow it to compel us to offer hospitality to those we encounter each day in a loving and gracious way. In the name of Jesus and through the work of the Holy Spirit. Amen.

31. COMMUNITY

WARREN SCHUH

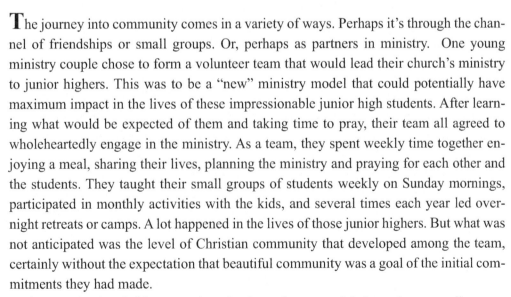

The journey into community comes in a variety of ways. Perhaps it's through the channel of friendships or small groups. Or, perhaps as partners in ministry. One young ministry couple chose to form a volunteer team that would lead their church's ministry to junior highers. This was to be a "new" ministry model that could potentially have maximum impact in the lives of these impressionable junior high students. After learning what would be expected of them and taking time to pray, their team all agreed to wholeheartedly engage in the ministry. As a team, they spent weekly time together enjoying a meal, sharing their lives, planning the ministry and praying for each other and the students. They taught their small groups of students weekly on Sunday mornings, participated in monthly activities with the kids, and several times each year led overnight retreats or camps. A lot happened in the lives of those junior highers. But what was not anticipated was the level of Christian community that developed among the team, certainly without the expectation that beautiful community was a goal of the initial commitments they had made.

The team leader vividly remembered a time when one of their mothers, a godly woman of the Word and prayer, joined them for one of their team's weeknight eating, sharing, and planning times. With godly wisdom, the mom urged the team to "remember to enjoy and cherish this community that you all are experiencing together, because it is uncommon and will not often be repeated in your lifetime."

Of course, given the youthfulness of the team, they thought this older voice was jaded, and at the time they didn't realize how easy and natural the experience of deep Christian community could be. But, over time and experience shared together as a team, they found she was absolutely correct. The experience of healthy, deep, refreshing Christian community is relatively rare and it is certainly not formulaic. While no one is by any means an expert in community, many have thought much about it and done much to pursue it. Here are a few observations that might be helpful in your own journey to deeper community:

1. We were created to be in and thrive in community. "It is not good for the man to be alone" (Genesis 2:18) We are created in the image of God who IS community: Father, Son and Holy Spirit.

2. The church was always intended to be the model of healthy, God-honoring community, and this may well be the most effective window through which the world will see God's love. (John 17:20-23)

3. Christian community is not automatic, cheap, or easy. While there are occasional "surprise" experiences of deep community, it is most often found in the context of committed time together, intentional relational development, vulnerability, honesty, and graciousness. In addition, working side by side to accomplish a larger Kingdom goal seems to be fertile ground in which community flourishes.

4. Christian community is a core reality of the blessing that is meant to be ours as God's children both in this life and in life everlasting. As such, it is worth the pursuit.

Above all else, the depth of one's soul impacts the depth of one's community. The pursuit of God and godliness individually helps to spur on the love of God and the desire to live God-honoring lives together. May your journey into Christian community be richly blessed!

"How good and pleasant it is when God's people live together in unity. It is like precious oil poured on the head, running down on the beard...for there the LORD bestows his blessing, even life forevermore."
—Psalm 133

"The more genuine and the deeper our community becomes, the more will everything else between us recede, the more clearly and purely will Jesus Christ and his work become the one and only thing that is vital between us. We have one another only through Christ, but through Christ we do have one another, wholly, for eternity."
—Dietrich Bonhoeffer, Life Together

"There are many things which a person can do alone, but being a Christian is not one of them. As the Christian life is, above all things, a state of union with Christ, and of union of his followers with one another. Love of the brethren is inseparable from love of God."
—William T. Ham

HEART WITH LOVING HEART UNITED
A HYMN BY NICOLAUS LUDWIG, COUNT VON ZINZENDORF, 1723

Heart with loving heart united, met to know God's holy will.
Let his love in us ignited more and more our spirits fill.
He the head, we are his members, we reflect the light he is.
He the master, we disciples, he is ours and we are his.

May we all so love each other and all selfish claims deny,
so that each one for the other will not hesitate to die.
Even so our Lord has loved us, for our lives he gave his life.
Still he grieves and still he suffers, for our selfishness and strife.

Since, O Lord, you have demanded that our lives your love should show,
so we wait to be commanded forth into your world to go.
Kindle in us love's compassion so that ev'ryone may see
in our fellowship the promise of a new humanity.

REFLECTION QUESTIONS

The American mindset tends toward making heroes out of "Lone Ranger" types. How does this tendency impact our concept of community? Has it influenced your perspective?

If you were to pursue a deepening level of community with fellow believers, what life-style changes would likely be necessary? What time commitments might change?

When you have experienced times of meaningful spiritual community during your life, what were the circumstances and contributing factors that facilitated those times?

Who are those in your life whom you might intentionally invite to live more of life together? Perhaps you might look for a diverse group of believers to live alongside and learn from. How is God nudging you?

SPIRITUAL PRACTICES

Each day this coming week, read John 17:20-23 and consider the implications of Jesus' prayer for your life.

If you have a group of fellow believers you meet with regularly, consider taking the next month to talk together about the experiences of community you have approached in the past and to thank God for those gifts. Decide on a couple of intentional steps you could take to deepen community with this group.

If you are not currently gathering regularly with a small group of believers, consider asking two or three friends to meet with you weekly for the next month or so to investigate together what the Bible says about community and the resulting implications for your lives today.

A Prayer of Illumination:

Gracious Father, thank you for loving us so deeply and inviting us into eternal community as sons and daughters. Jesus, thank you for making holy community possible and for initiating the experience of true community among your brothers and sisters here on earth. Holy Spirit, thank you for the ongoing bond of brotherly love you facilitate among us as we follow your promptings. Guide us more fully, we pray, into the realities of the true Christian community you desire for us. Amen.

32. COMPASSION

GAYLE HEASLIP

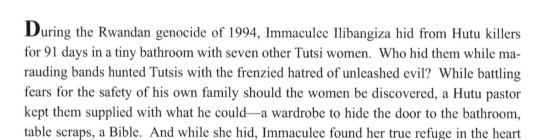

During the Rwandan genocide of 1994, Immaculee Ilibangiza hid from Hutu killers for 91 days in a tiny bathroom with seven other Tutsi women. Who hid them while marauding bands hunted Tutsis with the frenzied hatred of unleashed evil? While battling fears for the safety of his own family should the women be discovered, a Hutu pastor kept them supplied with what he could—a wardrobe to hide the door to the bathroom, table scraps, a Bible. And while she hid, Immaculee found her true refuge in the heart of the Lord, who is full of compassion-- "…the force of his love flowed through me like a sacred river, cleansing my soul and easing my mind."

Sometimes compassion rises spontaneously; sometimes it is formed over time as we ponder the struggles of others living alongside us in a broken world. However it comes, compassion is a response that is experienced viscerally. Scripturally, it means "to have the bowels yearn," to be deeply moved from the seat of our emotions.

Also translated as God's "tender mercies," compassion in the earthly life of Jesus always resulted in some concrete act as a response to being deeply moved. So, he cured the sick within the crowds (Matthew 9:36), healed blind men (Matthew 20:34) and lepers (Mark 1:41), taught the multitudes when he saw them "like sheep without a shepherd" (Mark 6:34), and raised a widow's only son (Luke 7:13). In the parables, compassion is the word Jesus used when he painted the landscapes of a father yearning for reconciliation with a prodigal son, of a king forgiving his servant an immense debt, of a Samaritan who generously cared for an injured stranger.

Compassion is the place where a heart formed in contemplation, in quietness and alone with God, moves back again into the larger sphere of God's love for the world, where it intersects and identifies with the needs of others and leads to concrete action.

Having been brought into the embrace of God by his grace alone, having rested within his arms as his beloved sons and daughters, having seen in Scripture what compassion looks like as it rises from inward depths to spill over into acts of mercy, we are opened up to offer this same great welcome and generosity of God to others. Compassion becomes the refracted light of glory, the sword that penetrates hearts of stone, the song of welcome to a lost and wandering people.

May we surrender wholeheartedly to this great God whose compassion identified with our brokenness and offered his tender mercies to us in the person of Christ.

"But you, Lord, are a compassionate and gracious God,
slow to anger, abounding in love and faithfulness."
—Psalm 86:15

"Finally, all of you, be like-minded, be sympathetic,
love one another, be compassionate and humble. Do not repay evil with evil
or insult with insult. On the contrary, repay evil with blessing,
because to this you were called so that you may inherit a blessing."
—1 Peter 3:8-9

"If you see the needy and bring him home, your limbs are the weapons of justice."
—Ambrose of Milan

THE LOVE OF GOD
A HYMN BY FREDERICK M. LEHMAN, 1917

The love of God is greater far
Than tongue or pen can ever tell.
It goes beyond the highest star
And reaches to the lowest hell.

The guilty pair, bowed down with care,
God gave His Son to win;
His erring child He reconciled
And pardoned from his sin.

O love of God, how rich and pure!
How measureless and strong!
It shall forevermore endure—
The saints' and angels' song.

Could we with ink the ocean fill,
And were the skies of parchment made;
Were every stalk on earth a quill,
And every man a scribe by trade;

To write the love of God above
Would drain the ocean dry;
Nor could the scroll contain the whole,
Though stretched from sky to sky.

REFLECTION QUESTIONS

What rises within you when you consider the compassion of the Lord for you personally? How did he identify with your needs on the cross? Are you aware of any needs that you cannot personally meet now? How might the Lord's compassion for you anchor you in his love until that need is met?

To what issues, events, or people are you regularly drawn to offer resources? When has your attention been surprisingly drawn to a place of need?

Have you felt some internal resistance to this? Sit quietly with the resistance in the Lord's deep and loving knowledge of you. What rises up from with your thoughts and emotions? Continue to explore any internal obstacles to being moved with compassion.

SPIRITUAL PRACTICES

Reflect on those times in your life when you experienced the compassion of the Lord directly or through others. Thank him for each of those experiences. Read Psalm 145:8-9; ask him to enlarge your capacity to move with his compassion on behalf of others.

Choose one or more of the references above from the Gospels. Place yourself within the narrative from the viewpoint of each person in the story. Notice your internal responses, and sit quietly before the Lord with them.

Make a commitment, when you are next moved with compassion for another, to ask the Lord for his wisdom and then to respond with concrete action, being willing to offer both heartfelt prayer and your time, presence, or resources.

A Prayer of Illumination:
Lord, your compassion is far greater than my capacity to receive or to give in like measure. Enfold me in your heart, whose boundaries embrace all who suffer with spiritual and material needs, for there I will not be discouraged or tempted to pull back in fear or judgment. In the freedom of knowing that I am daily crowned with your compassion, move me from deep within to love others extravagantly and so reveal the glory that is yours alone. Amen.

33. LISTENING TO GOD'S WORD

JEREMY STEFANO

When things get serious, parents say to their children: "Now listen to me." This is intended to convey that something more than listening is being required. Mom or dad is calling forth a certain kind of attentiveness that will result in tangible evidence of consent to their words. They are expecting that their words will bring about change in the attitude or actions of their children.

Jesus uses a distinctive phrase recorded in the Gospels: "If anyone has ears to hear, let him hear" (Mark 4:23). This is a kind of riddle not unlike the thing parents say to their children. It is a way Jesus has of bidding true listeners to heed his Word. Among the multitudes of people who heard him speak, only some were listening in a way that would allow a proper hearing of his words. "Let him hear!" can come as a command that makes the hearing Jesus requires possible. What if it is a word spoken to open ears up, so that his words will fall upon the ground of listening hearts?

Much of the time we listen to Scripture with the mindset of learning what to do. This is certainly an appropriate kind of engagement with God's Word. When this involves the extraction of a principle from the text and applying it in some practical way, there are benefits as the Christian seeks to implement godly values into their life. There are also limits to this method that can obstruct a deeper hearing, if it reduces all Scripture reading to the perpetual application of principles in one's life. This approach can unwittingly encourage the risk of reducing the gospel to a form of legalism.

When Jesus' pronouncement "Let him hear" falls on the listening ear, something is awakened in the heart. Jesus is calling forth something prior to and beyond any human ability. What is necessary is not a way of listening to God's Word simply to take charge of finding a principle to apply to life. There is also a way to wait with God's Word that allows the Word to be wrought in one's life. Obedience to God does not always mean doing something for God. Obedience requires a yielding of the will that consents to his Word being done in us.

Perhaps Abraham and Sarah can serve as an example: we all know that when this man and woman of faith took the promise of God concerning a son into their own hands, it was not the fulfillment of that Word that resulted. Rather, when they were able to rest in the promise, God's intended fulfillment was brought about in them. This type of reception of God's Word is poignantly expressed in the simple consent of Mary, the mother of Jesus: "Let it be done to me according to your word." Let us seek out opportunities to let God's Word be done in us, by taking time to listen with the ears of the heart, willing to receive that which is sown by the Sower of the Word of life.

"This is my Son, whom I love. Listen to him!"
—Mark 9:7

*"What hinders me from hearing is that I am taken up with other things.
I am devoted to things, to service, to convictions, and God may say what
He likes but I do not hear Him."*
—Oswald Chambers, My Utmost for His Highest

MASTER SPEAK! THY SERVANT HEARETH
A HYMN BY FRANCES RIDLEY HAVERGAL (1836-1879)

Master, speak! Thy servant heareth, Waiting for Thy gracious word,
Longing for Thy voice that cheereth, Master, let it now be heard.
I am listening, Lord, for Thee. What hast Thou to say to me?

Often through my heart is pealing, Many another voice than Thine
Many an unwilled echo stealing, From the walls of this Thy shrine.
Let Thy longed for accents fall, Master, speak! and silence all.

Master, speak! and make me ready, When Thy voice is truly heard
With obedience glad and steady, Still to follow every word.
I am listening, Lord, for Thee: Master, speak, oh, speak to me!

Speak to me by name, O Master, Let me know it is to me;
Speak, that I may follow faster, ith a step more firm and free,
Where the Shepherd leads the flock, In the shadow of the Rock!

REFLECTION QUESTIONS

What does Jesus mean when he affirms that man cannot live by bread alone, but that we are supplied by every word that comes from the mouth of God (Matthew 4:4)?

What clutters your heart, hindering your capacity to receive God's Word?

How does God generally work in you, equipping you to tangibly "do" his Word?

What patterns of your past or present may be hindering your ability to listen deeply to God's Word?

SPIRITUAL PRACTICES

Pay attention to the strategy of the enemy in your life to snatch away the seed of God's Word from your heart. Note the hindrances to which you are most inclined to capitulate.

Yielding one's heart can be hard. Find ways to say yes to God in the small, sometimes surprising, things/gifts/opportunities of an ordinary day.

After reading from Scripture, find occasion sometimes not only to ponder what the text means, but also simply to wait and receive the Word as a work God is doing in your heart.

Ask God to show you how he has fulfilled his Word in you.

A Prayer of Illumination:
Speak Lord, your servant is listening. Amen.

34. WITHHOLDING JUDGMENT

BR. DAVID VRYHOF, SSJE

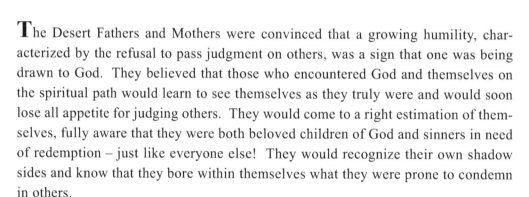

The Desert Fathers and Mothers were convinced that a growing humility, characterized by the refusal to pass judgment on others, was a sign that one was being drawn to God. They believed that those who encountered God and themselves on the spiritual path would learn to see themselves as they truly were and would soon lose all appetite for judging others. They would come to a right estimation of themselves, fully aware that they were both beloved children of God and sinners in need of redemption – just like everyone else! They would recognize their own shadow sides and know that they bore within themselves what they were prone to condemn in others.

Refusing to judge is a common theme in the desert tradition. Once in a monastery there was an assembly on account of a fallen brother. The fathers spoke; only Abba Pior kept silent. Afterward he stood up, took a sack, filled it with sand, and carried it on his shoulder. Meanwhile he held in front of him a little basket with a tiny amount of sand. The fathers asked him what that meant, and he answered, "This sack with all the sand is my sins. I have put them behind me so that they won't worry me, and I won't weep over them. And behold, the few errors of my brother are in front of me, and I say all sorts of things to condemn him. It is not right to do so. Rather I should carry my own in front of me and think about them and beg God to forgive them." Then the fathers stood up and said, "Truly, this the way of salvation."

Passing judgment on others makes us blind to our own mistakes. Jesus asked, "Why do you see the speck in your neighbor's eye, but do not notice the log in your own eye? Or how can you say to your neighbor, 'Friend, let me take out the speck in your eye,' when you yourself do not see the log in your own eye? You hypocrite, first take the log out of your own eye, and then you will see clearly to take the speck out of your neighbor's eye." (Luke 6:41,42)

For the Desert Fathers and Mothers, refusing to pass judgment was not only the by-product of a life of genuine asceticism; it was also the way to inner peace. Judging gives us no rest. For even while we are condemning the other, we unconsciously sense that we ourselves are not perfect. When we choose to withhold judgment, we allow others to be as they are, and in this way, we too can be ourselves.

Refraining from judgment acknowledges two things: First, we too are capable of making mistakes. And second, if we are honest, we do not know the person or the situation well enough to assume the role of judge. The Rule of the Society of St. John the Evangelist states, "In silence we honor the mystery present in the hearts of [other people]. Only God knows them as they truly are and in silence we learn to let go of the curiosity, presumption, and condemnation which pretends to penetrate the mystery of their hearts..." (SSJE Rule, chapter 27).

When we refuse to speak disdainfully of others, we give ourselves a chance to look on them without prejudice. When we withhold judgment and criticism, it becomes possible to see others with compassion and sympathy. We know deep in our hearts that we are all in need of compassion – God's compassion, and the compassion of our fellow human beings. Refraining from judgment allows us to appreciate that we all share this need.

"Do not judge, and you will not be judged; do not condemn, and you will not be condemned. Forgive, and you will be forgiven."
—Luke 6:37

"If you judge people, you have no time to love them."
——Mother Teresa

THERE'S A WIDENESS IN GOD'S MERCY
A HYMN BY FREDRICK WILLIAM FABER(1814-1863)

There's a wideness in God's mercy like the wideness of the sea;
there's a kindness in his justice, which is more than liberty.
There is welcome for the sinner, and more graces for the good;
there is mercy with the Savior; there is healing in his blood.

There is no place where earth's sorrows are more felt than up in heaven;
there is no place where earth's failings have such kindly judgment given.
There is plentiful redemption in the blood that has been shed;
there is joy for all the members in the sorrows of the Head.

For the love of God is broader than the measure of the mind;
and the heart of the Eternal is most wonderfully kind.
If our love were but more faithful, we should take him at his word;
and our life would be thanksgiving for the goodness of the Lord.

REFLECTION QUESTIONS

Pray with one or more of these Gospel stories: The Pharisee and the Publican (Luke 18:9-14); A Sinful Woman Anoints Jesus (Luke 7:36-50); Jesus Refuses to Condemn a Woman (John 8:2-11). What can you learn from these stories?

How can the conscious practice of silence help curb our tendency to judge others?

The Baptismal Covenant in the *Book of Common Prayer* states that one of our obligations as Christians is "to respect the dignity of every human being" (BCP, p. 305). What practical implications might this have for you?

SPIRITUAL PRACTICES

Consider the person(s) or situation(s) about which you are most likely to complain. Examine your thoughts and feelings towards them. Ask for the grace to see them in a new light and to speak of them in a new way.

Consider the labels you have assigned to people in your life. What adjectives are you likely to use when you think of them? From where did this label come? Can you take a fresh look at them without this label?

In what ways have you judged yourself? Are there labels you have affixed to yourself that reflect self-disdain? Look at yourself objectively, free of these negative labels.

A Prayer of Illumination:
Lord, awaken my heart to a deeper awareness of my propensity to judge another, and free me from uninformed prejudice and pride, so that I may look into the eyes of others as you humbly, lovingly, and graciously see them today. In the name of Jesus, Amen.

35. BROKEN AND WHOLE

STEPHEN A. MACCHIA

———◆———

Embrace our brokenness? Find strength in our weakness? Allow God to redeem our pain? When our interior world is tethering at the seams, we don't want to go there! But it is exactly within those questions where we meet God at a deeper, more grace-filled place. We know we are broken and in need of God, and amidst that more authentic geography of the soul, we become more certain of our belovedness in God's eyes. Because of that incredible truth, "you are dearly loved by God," we are free from the bondage of our brokenness, that "I am deeply sinful and in need of God." Wholeness is on the horizon, when the unconditional love of God is what's called upon to heal, redeem, and restore.

The primary source of our brokenness is not necessarily our vocation, our calling, our experiences, or our relationships. Instead, it arises from the raw material of our daily lives within each of those categories, and it arises when coping mechanisms which had worked before no longer are fruitful. When we confront insurmountable challenges we thought we could "fix,"and we discover instead the reality that they may in fact be irreparable, we are left in the dark. When the wounds of our distant past rear their ugly heads, it's best to seek professional help and enlist the care of an excellent therapist. When we cling to the promise that the truth will set us free...from any number of areas of bondage or uncertainty…then we are changed from the inside out. Our brokenness, in light of God's mercy, leads redemptively to our wholeness in God.

It takes brokenness to get us out of the fog of leading and serving and living from a perceived place of vigor and vitality and into genuine wholeness. What we have seen in others whom we emulate as strong leaders was in fact more of a façade. They too had bruises left unattended; they too had sin patterns that eventually took a toll; they too had need for God to attend to their brokenness and restore them to his original intention. They too had pretense and posturing which only God could heal and redeem. We simply join their ranks.

When we discover hard truths about ourselves, it's like unlocking biblical truth which lead you down the pathway of an emancipated soul. After discovering your brokenness, acknowledging its reality in your heart, mind and soul…it's best to gently release it into the hands of a loving God who is always more than willing to carry it for you. And, more importantly, God is desirous of redeeming all of your brokenness for his glory. When that realization settles into the deepest crevices of your worn and weary soul, new life begins to emerge. You will become a completely different person: still in the process of redemption, but experiencing the joy of wholeness in Christ like never before.

What are you holding on to today that is the true and broken you? Are you crippled by the fear of admitting your brokenness and the brokenness that others have inflicted upon you? Be encouraged toward owning, naming, and then releasing your brokenness into the hands of a very loving heavenly Father. God himself is there to hold and comfort you no matter what you carry today. Let his love enfold you and heal you from the inside out…that's exactly what God is all about!

"He gives strength to the weary and increases the power of the weak."
—Isaiah 40:29

" 'My grace is sufficient for you, for my power is made perfect in weakness.'
Therefore, I will boast all the more gladly about my weaknesses, so that Christ's power
may rest on me...For when I am weak, then I am strong."
—2 Corinthians 12:9, 10

MY FAITH LOOKS UP TO THEE
A HYMN BY RAY PALMER, 1830

My faith looks up to thee,
thou Lamb of Calvary,
Savior divine!
Now hear me while I pray;
take all my guilt away.
O let me from this day
be wholly thine!

May thy rich grace impart
strength to my fainting heart,
my zeal inspire.
As thou hast died for me,
O may my love to thee
pure, warm, and changeless be,
a living fire!

While life's dark maze I tread
and griefs around me spread,
be thou my guide;
bid darkness turn to day,
wipe sorrow's tears away,
nor let me ever stray
from thee aside.

When life's swift race is run,
death's cold work almost done,
be near to me.
Blest Savior, then, in love
fear and distrust remove.
O bear me safe above,
redeemed and free!

REFLECTION QUESTIONS

Do you believe wholeheartedly that you are a dearly loved child of God? Have you received the gift of God's grace, mercy, and forgiveness found solely in Jesus Christ? If so, what stands in the way of your living an abundant life today?

When you consider your own brokenness, what comes to the forefront of your heart and mind? Suffering, pain, heartache, sinfulness, imperfections?

What would it look like for you to hand over your brokenness and weakness to God today?

If necessary, are you willing to seek the help of a soul companion to help guide you forward?

SPIRITUAL PRACTICES

Imagine Jesus sitting with you and a dear friend. What words would Jesus use to describe you to your friend as a dearly loved and forgiven child of God? Write these words or phrases down on paper (use words that describe your personhood, not just your gifts, talents, and abilities).

Prayerfully consider the brokenness that others have inflicted upon you. Write out a prayer of forgiveness, and consider ways to bless (rather than retaliate) them in return.

Share honestly and offer a listening ear to a trusted friend. What area of brokenness or weakness would you like God to redeem for his glory and purpose in your life today?

A Prayer of Illumination:
Father, hold me gently in your love's sanctifying and transforming embrace. Jesus, gracefully forgive and redeem my brokenness. Holy Spirit, renew your work in my heart and life, and may your strength emerge from my weakness. All for the sake of your Kingdom and the glory of your Name. Amen.

36. CONFLICT

DIANA CURREN BENNETT

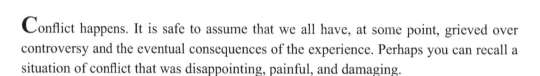

Conflict happens. It is safe to assume that we all have, at some point, grieved over controversy and the eventual consequences of the experience. Perhaps you can recall a situation of conflict that was disappointing, painful, and damaging.

Conflict is stressful. Yet conflict can also be beneficial. Ultimately, God shapes conflict when the need for resolution is recognized and experienced in a healthy process.

As an example, two good and close friends started a Bible study ministry. With much prayer and thoughtful organization, the group grew--and enrollment became overwhelming. The weight of responsibilities mounted. Within a short period of time, it became evident that these two close friends possessed totally different styles of leadership--a discovery that caused high friction with their leadership. Frustration increased, and the relationship became threatened. How does one preserve the quality of ministry, value friendship, yet create an environment where both parties can fully utilize their spiritual gifts and thrive?

The clash was becoming destructive. With the fragility of this relationship, both leaders knew resolution was needed. The healthiest options for restoration became obvious. Personalities and leadership styles were probably not going to change quickly, if at all. Unrealized expectations and unexpressed hurtful feelings needed to be verbalized if reconciliation was to occur. Communication was guarded. It would have been easier for them to quit and do something else. But, knowing that it would please God and for the benefit of the thriving ministry, these two friends worked through various perceptions and responses to each other's leadership styles. It was the beginning of healthy resolution.

The friends decided to pray weekly with one another for the restoration of this long-lived friendship. It was hard, but it was significant. God moved in the difficult prayer time. The relationship was slowly salvaged. The experience taught an important lesson: it is not conflict that ruins a relationship, but the failure to understand how to correctly process and resolve the conflict.

Jesus caused conflict purely on the basis of who he was, especially among the Pharisees, who considered his presence a direct threat to their authority. There were times when he deliberately asked questions that resulted in conflict. This became a tool Jesus used to provoke his listeners and reveal their hearts. The disciples were no strangers to conflict, either – conflict over who was the greatest, their learning curve of faith, which constituents were worthy of Jesus' time, how to spend their time and money, even conflict at being publicly identified as Christ-followers. And, of course, it was conflict with religious leaders and even a fickle crowd that eventually resulted in Jesus' crucifixion. The cross redeemed it all.

And conflict is familiar to us as well. We strike at one another through disagreements of ideas and interests, we clash with different personalities and leadership styles, and we cause emotional scars while clinging to our personal hopes and expectations. The element of fear and the threat of change put us on the defensive, driving the desire to ignore, eliminate, or run from problematic situations. However the conflict is managed, it is always challenging and often painful. But God invites us to address conflict directly, openly, and with humility. Through the process, he refines us, and we learn valuable lessons about ourselves and others. Pray for wisdom as you seek resolution to the conflicts you face today.

Consider this basic approach to conflict as it occurs: a) name the conflict and identify the sources (issues, personalities, words spoken, etc.); b) bring the parties at hand together to give voice to their disagreement; c) be gentle and patient with one another; d) speak the truth in love; e) intervene as needed; f) prayerfully consider how best to resolve the conflict together; g) know when to give it time or to keep proceeding toward resolution. Always serve the conflicted with ample grace and mercy. Conflict is inevitable. Peace is the desire. Resolution and unity is the preferred outcome.

"Let us therefore make every effort to do what leads to peace and
to mutual edification." —
—Romans 14:19

"Conflict is not undesirable. It is of the very essence of life within
a community that values difference and honors the diversity of God's
creative design evidenced in humanity."
—Sam Portaro, Conflict and a Christian Life

LEAD ME, LORD
A HYMN BY SAMUEL S. WESLEY, 1861

Lead me, Lord, lead me in thy righteousness,
make thy way plain before my face.
For it is thou, Lord, thou, Lord, only,
that makest me dwell in safety.

Teach me, Lord, teach me truly how to live,
that I may come to know thee,
and in thy presence serve thee with gladness,
and sing songs of praise to thy glory.

REFLECTION QUESTIONS

As we consider our reactions to controversy, how do you respond when conflict presents itself?

How did your family handle conflict when you were young? In what way have you adopted the model you experienced in your early years? ("Just ignore it," "It's just the way she is," "You're right so forget it," "Just move on")

More often than not, conflict is seen as a win-lose situation. This view is destructive and is to be avoided at all costs. When managed properly, conflict can be used to great advantage. How do you see present conflict as beneficial to your spiritual growth?

As you consider how Jesus resolved conflicts with and among his followers, what are the Christ-like attributes of resolution you seek to embody in your life?

The early church was ripe for conflict. When Pentecost came upon them, in Acts 2, the church was united, fruitful, and filled up with God. What do you long for today in your church?

SPIRITUAL PRACTICES

EXAMEN: What comes to mind as displeasing to God with your response to a conflict at hand? Sit quietly and ask God to reveal to you what one step you can take to start the resolution process.

HUMILITY: Examine your heart, soul, and mind within this conflict. This requires a humble spirit. In what way have you or have you not been willing to be humble and loving during this conflict?

LISTEN: Ask yourself if you have listened well to the person with whom you are in conflict. Have you listened to the Holy Spirit's urging? If not, ask God to reveal to you what he has planned for the beginning of resolution. Be obedient to what you hear.

PRAY: As God reveals to you how you have contributed to a conflict, what is he inviting you to consider as one who pursues peace and reconciliation?

NOTICE: Watch how the Spirit of God brings unity in the body of Christ. Celebrate when conflicts are resolved. Work prayerfully and intentionally toward desired oneness and collective unity always and in every conflicted circumstance.

A Prayer of Illumination:
God of forgiveness, peace, and grace, please pour down the Holy Spirit on me as I listen, reflect, and discern wise actions in responding to disappointing conflict. Help me to respond with humility and trust. May my actions be pleasing to you and reflect the image of Jesus, in whose name I pray. Amen.

37. FORGIVENESS IS A CHOICE

STEPHEN A. MACCHIA

There is nothing easy about forgiveness. It's one of those areas of daily life we'd rather live without. Who among us likes to say "I'm sorry" or "I was wrong" or "Please forgive me"? But, without these life-saving and relational-essential phrases coming from our lips, we are tormented by things like bitterness, anger, resentment, frustration, and angst. Too many in our world accept these negative responses as givens, and that's to our collective shame. Isn't it time we all grow up - in Christ - and more freely offer forgiveness to one another - in Christ?

The need for forgiveness is universal, because conflict is inevitable. How we respond to our relational conflicts is in our hands and hearts to determine. Psychologists generally define forgiveness as a conscious, deliberate decision to release feelings of resentment or vengeance toward a person or group who has harmed you, regardless of whether they actually deserve your forgiveness. The general definition fits all fallen human beings worldwide. Therefore, no one is exempt from its consideration.

The choice is yours: what will it be? In the realm of the soul, forgiveness is central to one's spiritual vitality. Praying into how best to live as a forgiving person is of utmost importance. Learning how to let go of needing to be right, releasing our anger, bitterness, and thoughts of revenge, and walking in freedom and joy, is hard to do. Why?

Because it requires that we become more grace-filled, compassionate, understanding, empathetic, prayerful, and ultimately merciful in our relational interactions. All of this is made possible in Christ. All of this is rooted in the heart of the forgiver. Is forgiveness in your heart?

The fact of the matter is: we have been extravagantly forgiven by God for all the ways we've stiff-armed him in our lives, and all of us have done so to one extent or another. We are therefore invited by God to continuously forgive as we've been forgiven; to love as we've first been loved; to offer grace as we've received grace. That's what the message of the cross and the resurrection life is all about. Our prayer is to be: forgive us our trespasses as we forgive those who trespass against us. Our example is in Christ: Father, forgive them, for they know not what they are doing.

It is completely possible to forgive someone yet still feel hurt, as Jesus felt saddened by those who denied, betrayed, and ultimately left him to suffer alone in the garden and on the cross. As Jesus offered to Peter, there is room for one who denies another to earn the trust back. Peter, after his denial, reaffirms his love for Jesus three times over, and Jesus welcomes him back with a loving embrace of grace. But, for us, forgiveness doesn't always lead to renewed trust, or even full reconciliation. It's the forgiveness of a forgiver that sets a heart free to live, love, and serve with joy.

Forgiveness is a choice: ask for it when necessary; receive it when it's offered; encourage it when it's ignored. Refusing it will lead to deeper pain; refusing to offer it will keep you in bondage; refusing to see the need for it will lead you into deeper darkness. So, forget what you can; release what you must; and restore what you may. Express compassion, empathy, and mercy, instead of grief, suffering, and brokenness. Humble yourself. Apologize. Pray. Forgive. The longer you go without forgiveness, the longer it will take to rebuild trust and pursue reconciliation. There's really no better way to live. Make the right choice today.

"Be kind and compassionate to one another, forgiving each other,
just as in Christ God forgave you."
—Ephesians 4:32

"Bear with each other and forgive one another if any of you has
a grievance against someone. Forgive as the Lord forgave you."
—Colossians 3:13

GOD OF GRACE AND GOD OF GLORY
A HYMN BY Harry Emerson Fosdick, 1930

God of grace and God of glory,
On your people pour your power;
Crown your ancient church's story,
Bring its bud to glorious flower.
Grant us wisdom, grant us courage,
For the facing of this hour, for the facing of this hour.

Lo, the hosts of evil round us
Scorn the Christ, assail his ways!
From the fears that long have bound us
Free our hearts to faith and praise.
Grant us wisdom, grant us courage,
For the living of these days, for the living of these days.

Cure your children's warring madness;
Bend our pride to your control;
Shame our wanton, selfish gladness,
Rich in things and poor in soul.
Grant us wisdom, grant us courage,
Lest we miss your kingdom's goal, lest we miss your kingdom's goal.

Save us from weak resignation
To the evils we deplore;
Let the gift of your salvation
Be our glory evermore.
Grant us wisdom, grant us courage,
Serving you whom we adore, serving you whom we adore.

REFLECTION QUESTIONS

Is there a relational conflict in your life that needs prayerful attention? If you were to rewrite the narrative, how would the conflict have been avoided?

Consider prayerfully the phrase in the hymn above, "Cure your children's warring madness; bend our pride to your control." In what ways does your lack of forgiveness toward another look and feel like "madness"? If God were to "bend your pride to his control," what would that look like in this relational conflict?

When is offering forgiveness easier for you? more challenging for you?

Are you waiting for someone in your life to apologize? What if it never comes?

In what way is the mandate to forgive linked to your difficulty in releasing the need to be right, and in an unwillingness to lovingly and humbly forgive someone who wronged you? How can you embrace forgiveness without the preferred trust or reconciliation?

SPIRITUAL PRACTICES

Journal about a recent conflict and resultant forgiveness. Write out your role in the resolution, restoration, and reconciliation.

Memorize a verse of Scripture that refers to forgiveness. Consider Ephesians 4:32 and Colossians 3:13.

Read Psalm 51. What were David's prayerful words of confession, the forgiveness offered to him by God, and the results of a renewal of his heart? What's required of us in offering words of confession, words of forgiveness and assurance, and words of compassionate mercy to others?

Prayerfully consider Jesus' imperative of forgiveness in the Lord's Prayer (Matthew 6:5-15; Luke 11:1-4).

Read Jesus' parable on forgiveness in Matthew 18:21-35. Notice any sense of conviction, counsel, or correction as it relates to your heart of forgiveness and grace.

A Prayer of Illumination

Father, help us to extend forgiveness to others in our lives who have wronged us, to release the need to be right, and to humbly offer mercy and grace in your name. Give us the courage to admit when we are the one who's been in the wrong, and empower us with the ability to voice our apology with sincerity. May we always look to Jesus as our example of unconditional acceptance and unhindered compassion to all who cross our path. And may our hearts become ever more forgiving toward all who cross our path. For the sake of your kingdom and the glory of your name, loving Father, gracious Savior, empowering Spirit. Amen.

CREATIVITY

38. CREATIVITY

RICK ANDERSON

You are a created being. Do you believe that? For most of us, that is a foundational truth that is easy to accept. But do you acknowledge that at your core you are also a creative being? Why is that truth more difficult to swallow? Pablo Picasso said, "Every child is an artist; the problem is staying an artist when you grow up." Maybe you are not a painter. Few people are. But, of course, you need not be an artist to be creative. Perhaps we need to think more creatively about what it means to be creative! Have you ever engaged in any of these activities? Story-telling, cooking, decorating, designing, modifying, painting, gardening, photography, poetry, woodworking, planning, pottery-making, imagining, sculpting, drawing, singing, writing, inventing, problem-solving, hospitality--the source of all of this is creativity.

Every human possesses creative faculties, having been made in God's image. But some are more alert to their creativity than others. See if you can identify yourself in one of these three profiles:

The Doubting Creative thinks, "I am just not a creative person." It is a tragedy that many adults have come to believe that there is not an ounce of creativity within them. Is that your story? Pause for a moment and try to identify where and when that notion began. What is likely absent is not creativity, but the confidence to express yourself creatively. When was that taken from you? To deny or ignore your creativity is to miss out on an element of God's image that resides in you!

The Dormant Creative thinks, "I used to have creative outlets in my life, but not so much lately." Maybe you have just gotten busy with more "productive" pursuits over the years, and creative activities that you used to enjoy have gone by the wayside. What did you lose along the way? It can be recovered! Your creative spirit is merely dormant--always ready to be awakened.

The Delighted Creative thinks, "I love to be creative. It's just part of who I am." Don't take your creativity for granted. Your awareness of it is a gift. Perhaps you've been affirmed for your creativity where others have been bruised by criticism or some other harmful experience. How can you confirm and call out the creativity in others?

So how does creativity impact our spiritual formation journey? Through your creative spirit you reflect the very nature of God in a way no other living thing does. Exploring that creative nature could awaken you to connect with your Creator in new and unexpected ways. The creation and appreciation of beauty and design draws you into kindred fellowship with God.

Whatever form your creativity takes, it is a life-bringing act, and you reflect the Creator when you use it. Explore the boundaries of your creativity and look for new ways to turn it loose!

"Blessed are those whose help is the God of Jacob, whose hope is in the Lord their God. He is the Maker of heaven and earth, the sea, and everything in them—he remains faithful forever."
—Psalm 146:5-6

"Though typically associated only with artists and children, creativity partially reflects the image of God within each of us. It is one strand of our divine DNA. The other strand is love, which is enormously creative. Woven together in a double helix, creativity and love compose the soul's purpose in life while providing the tools to mirror our Creator."
—Karla M. Kincannon, Creativity and Divine Surprise

ALL CREATURES OF OUR GOD AND KING
A HYMN BY ST. FRANCIS OF ASSISI (1225), trans. WILLIAM H. DRAPER
(Verses 1, 2, 3, 5)

All creatures of our God and King,
Lift up your voice and with us sing, O praise him, Alleluia!
Thou burning sun with golden beam,
And silver moon with softer gleam,
O praise him, O praise him, Alleluia! Alleluia! Alleluia!

Thou rushing wind that art so strong,
Ye clouds that sail in Heaven along, O praise him, Alleluia!
Thou rising moon, in praise rejoice,
Ye lights of evening, find a voice!
O praise him, O praise him, Alleluia! Alleluia! Alleluia!

Thou flowing water, pure and clear,
Make music for thy Lord to hear, O praise him, Alleluia!
Thou fire so masterful and bright,
That givest man both warmth and light,
O praise him, O praise him, Alleluia! Alleluia! Alleluia!

Let all things their Creator bless,
And worship Him in humbleness, O praise him, Alleluia!
Praise, praise the Father, praise the Son,
And praise the Spirit, Three in One!
O praise him, O praise him, Alleluia! Alleluia! Alleluia!

REFLECTION QUESTIONS

Candidly answer this question: Are you a creative person? What internal resistance do you sense in answering, "Yes!"?

What is the work/play balance in your life currently? Is there a connection between your sense of play and your awareness of the creativity within you?

What types of places or experiences put you into a creative mood, and how can you foster your creative spirit? How can you revisit those places or experiences more often in the future?

Can you think of a time when you created something that gave you joy? As you reflect back, do you have any sense of sharing in God's "it is good" delight?

SPIRITUAL PRACTICES

Take a blank sheet or journal page and list as many ideas as you can for creative expressions. Stretch yourself to brainstorm beyond art and music (a batch of cookies and a travel itinerary are both "created" things).

Take a risk. Choose one of the creative activities you listed, and invite God to accompany you as you engage in it purely for the joy of sharing it together. Your Heavenly Father would love to share this fun and creative time with you!

Ask God to show you the ways in which you reflect his creative nature. Ask him also to show you any instances where your creativity has been stifled and to reveal his desire to set it free.

A Prayer of Illumination:
"Loving Source of all creativity, you have formed us to join you in the work of shaping a world that reflects your design for unity in diversity among all your creatures. I gladly give myself to this great charge and ask that you inspire in me holy creativity greater than I could ask or even imagine. Amen." (Rueben Job)

39. CREATION

JEREMY STEFANO

$\diamond$

The Living God is Lord of all by distinction of being the God who creates all. The importance of this assertion is that God brings into being what does not exist before, or without, his Word. There is no greater claim to divinity, to being God, than that of being the Creator. Consequently, all that does exist has its source in God: origin, from God; being, in God; and purpose, for God.

"It is the glory of God to conceal a matter," says Solomon, "and the glory of kings to search it out" (Proverbs 25:2). While the material of creation is evident to the senses, the laws that govern it are hidden from view. The beauty and splendor of the creation stir and enrapture the heart, shaping the humble soul in wonder and gratitude. Meanwhile, the faculty of human intellect is given to search out and ponder the principles by which such wonder is sustained. What "kingly" intellects have pondered and empirically confirmed is the presence of hidden, reliable, and predictable forces that are active within the natural order. These powers are so dependable that scientists and physicists call them laws. The *laws* of physics!

To settle the vexed Job, the God of Israel asks him if he was there when all came into existence. Then God presses further, inquiring whether Job had approved or enacted the laws by which all is governed: "Do you know the ordinances of the heavens, or fix their rule over the earth?" No, Job hadn't thought about that. God goes on: "Can you lift your voice to the clouds so that an abundance of water will cover you?" (Job 38:33-34). No again, it is not a human word that animates and orders all creation. It is none but God who governs, with the laws and statutes of his wisdom, embedded in the very fabric of the created order.

What is our response to such a Creator if not outright praise and exultation of him who is the Living God! How odd then that the uncovering of the laws of physics by the gifts of human reason should give credence to any denial of the existence of God the Creator. Perceiving and explaining something about the laws that move the clouds across the sky and that cause the rain to fall does not make God any less God! It is by his Word of power that everything exists, and by his rule that all things remain.

We worship God as the Creator not only by looking back to the beginning, but also by acknowledging the amazing reality of being upheld right now by the Word of his power (Hebrews 1:3). For the God who created all things promises to re-create the heavens and the earth. Faith in a God who has spoken all things into being, whose Word sustains all that is suspended in place, is solid ground for hope. This God, our God, has spoken again: "See, I am making all things new" (Revelation 21:5).

"Since the creation of the world God's invisible attributes, his eternal power and divine nature, have been clearly seen, being understood from what has been made, so that people are without excuse."
—Romans 1:20

"We believe in one God, the Father Almighty, Maker of heaven and earth, and of all things visible and invisible."
—The Nicene Creed, 381 A.D.

I SING THE MIGHTY POWER OF GOD
A HYMN BY ISAAC WATTS, 1715

I sing the mighty pow'r of God,
that made the mountains rise,
That spread the flowing seas abroad,
and built the lofty skies.
I sing the wisdom that ordained the sun
to rule the day;
The moon shines full at His command,
and all the stars obey.

I sing the goodness of the Lord,
who filled the earth with food,
Who formed the creatures through the Word,
and then pronounced them good.
Lord, how Thy wonders are displayed,
where'er I turn my eye,
If I survey the ground I tread,
or gaze upon the sky.

There's not a plant or flow'r below,
but makes Thy glories known,
And clouds arise, and tempests blow,
by order from Thy throne;
While all that borrows life from Thee
is ever in Thy care;
And everywhere that we can be,
Thou, God, art present there.

REFLECTION QUESTIONS

If God's invisible qualities are, in fact, clearly seen in what God has created, what qualities or attributes of God are being revealed in the created order around you?

What geographical or geological features most readily inspire you to worship the Living God?

How can it be that the sun and moon, birds and flowers give honor to God by being what they are, yet we can fail to do so by the powers of our reason and the hesitation of our heart?

SPIRITUAL PRACTICES

God's enemies detract from his being the Creator. Read Psalm 8 as a little one with a heart to praise him.

Take notice of those things that delight you in this creation, which you hope to enjoy with the Lord in his New Creation.

Write a psalm of your own that extols and worships God the Creator and Sustainer of all that is.

A Prayer of Illumination:
Lord God, how wonderful are Your works! How vast Your wisdom! In reverence we honor You, and with joy we celebrate all You are and all You do. Through Jesus Christ, our Lord. Amen.

40. CONTEMPLATIVE ARTISTIC EXPRESSION

STEPHEN A. MACCHIA

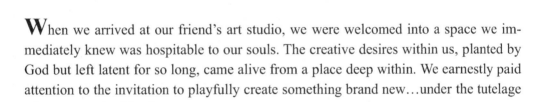

When we arrived at our friend's art studio, we were welcomed into a space we immediately knew was hospitable to our souls. The creative desires within us, planted by God but left latent for so long, came alive from a place deep within. We earnestly paid attention to the invitation to playfully create something brand new…under the tutelage of a trustworthy friend.

So, imagine this space…filled with natural light from windows on all sides. Overstuffed drawers packed with art supplies. Cubbies of colorful cones holding woolen yarns. A floor loom for weaving and tapestry. Bookshelves packed with contemplative readings and art books for inspiration. Two Amish-made hickory rockers inviting reflection or conversation. Mason jars filled with pencils and pens for drawing and calligraphy. A stained-glass mosaic and a watercolor painting in process. Framed art on the walls.

We sat as a small group of explorers at the large art table in the middle of the studio. And on that morning, through the realm of what our teacher called "artful prayer," we discovered a part of our true selves that brought us great joy. It was as if we were on a journey in a foreign country, with fellow pilgrims by our side--and a gracious guide pointing us down a delicious pathway of creative, enlightening, and renewing discovery.

We were instructed step by step to choose the first letter of a passage of Scripture that has been important to us recently. Inspired by the Celtic and Gothic illuminated alphabets, we learned how to embellish our chosen letter, paying attention to the smallest details and spaces of the letter with a slowing, restful, reflective posture. We listened to Scripture and quiet music in the background, while the foreground of artistic expression came alive in our midst. It was an amazing experience, one which we will never forget.

Since then, we haven't returned to our friend's studio, but instead we have rediscovered God's overwhelming "studio" of creation all around us. We've begun noticing – with renewed eyes – the beauty of God's creation: mountains, oceans, rivers, trees, flowers, birds, and clouds. With the help of a camera, we've been capturing sights that appeal to the senses and enliven the soul. We've been doodling, drawing, journaling, and noticing…holding rocks and twigs and shells and paying attention to the intricacies of God's design…listening afresh to the multiple dimensions of the stories of Scripture… praying attentively into the rhythms and themes of daily life.

And we've been discovering, along the way, that there are many other non-artists among us who are desirous of a growing depth of intimacy with Christ and are weary of the more mechanistic ways of getting there. The palate of creative expression is vast and endless! And it's within reach to all who long for a refreshingly new way of getting to know the Creator, Sustainer, Redeemer, and Transformer of our lives…God the Father, Jesus the Son, and the Spirit we call Holy.

"God saw all that he had made, and it was very good."
—Genesis 1:31

"The heavens declare the glory of God; the skies proclaim the work of his hands."
—Psalm 19:1

GOD MOVES IN A MYSTERIOUS WAY
A HYMN BY WILLIAM COWPER, 1774

God moves in a mysterious way
His wonders to perform;
He plants His footsteps in the sea
And rides upon the storm.

Deep in unfathomable mines
Of never failing skill
He treasures up His bright designs
And works His sov'reign will.

Ye fearful saints, fresh courage take;
The clouds ye so much dread
Are big with mercy and shall break
In blessings on your head.

Judge not the Lord by feeble sense,
But trust Him for His grace;
Behind a frowning providence
He hides a smiling face.

His purposes will ripen fast,
Unfolding every hour;
The bud may have a bitter taste,
But sweet will be the flow'r.

Blind unbelief is sure to err
And scan His work in vain;
God is His own interpreter,
And He will make it plain.

REFLECTION QUESTIONS

What do you like to do that brings out your "creative" side? What have you yet to experience but would love to pursue in this regard?

What would your "prayer closet" look like if you added a creative element to your biblical reflections and personal prayers?

How do your creative outlets remind you of God and return your heart to gratefully abiding in Christ and rejoicing in his trustworthiness?

In what way could your spiritual friendships or community add to their shared experiences as creative outlets of spiritual expression?

SPIRITUAL PRACTICES

Allow your creative side to emerge in your prayer closet, or on a retreat, or with a small group of friends…perhaps through visual or musical arts.

Consider taking a class or attending a workshop that helps you hone an artistic expression (painting, drawing, photography, calligraphy, poetry, learning a musical instrument), which could in turn enhance your spiritual disciplines and intimacy with Christ.

Go to the beach, walk in the woods, sit out under the night sky, or hike a mountain trail, and notice the many uniquely designed creative elements of this world that God has given for your enjoyment and his glory. Catalog your findings.

Sit reflectively and prayerfully with something you have created. Look at it with the Lord – aware of his abiding presence and peace. Enjoy this new creation together!

A Prayer of Illumination:
Loving Father, Creator of all that exists in this world, sustain and redeem us by your grace as we discover, enjoy, honor, and praise you for the delightful ways you abundantly love us and invite us to trust you in return. We want to notice you in our lives more attentively and prayerfully, so we humbly ask you to open the eyes of our prayerful hearts. May our transforming creativity come alive in new ways today, all for your honor and glory. We pray in your Spirit's power and in the name of your Son, our Savior, Jesus Christ. Amen.

41. SPACIOUSNESS

ANGELA WISDOM

———◇———

Would you describe your life with God as "open and expansive"? Those words sound incredibly inviting. Most of us long to live in spacious places. Wide-open landscapes offer fresh air to breathe and room to stretch. Something in our soul stirs when we experience spaciousness and beauty. However, for many believers, the landscapes of our lives don't look much different than the depleted, cluttered environments inhabited by our neighbors. Yet Jesus said, "I have come that they might have life and have it to the full." Do we dare believe that fullness of life is possible in Christ? Or is this only a hope for heaven?

An open and expansive life is lived from a place of abiding trust in God and his ways rather than from a place of fear, self-preservation, and self-sufficiency. It looks markedly different from the general culture. Rather than living on "auto pilot" or at the mercy of circumstances beyond our control, we take time and pause to re-focus our attention and our priorities in a way that helps us "keep in step with the Spirit" (Galatians 5:25).

Even in the complex culture of the New Testament church, Paul seemed convinced that a wide-open, spacious life was possible. To the church at Corinth he says: "Companions… please don't squander one bit of this marvelous life God has given us… I can't tell you how much I long for you to enter this wide-open, spacious life. We didn't fence you in. The smallness you feel comes from within you. Your lives aren't small, but you're living them in a small way. I'm speaking as plainly as I can and with great affection. Open up your lives. Live openly and expansively!" Of God, he says to the Colossians: "So spacious is he, so roomy, that everything of God finds its proper place in him without crowding. Not only that, but all the broken and dislocated pieces of the universe - people and things, animals and atoms - get properly fixed and fit together in vibrant harmonies…" (2 Corinthians 6:1, 11; Colossians 1:19-20, *The Message*)

When a natural environment has been polluted or depleted of valuable resources, or has been choked by invasive species of plants and animals, remediation is needed if that environment is to return to a state of sustainability. Such efforts involve attending to the soil, ground and surface water, as well as flora and fauna. It requires an initial commitment to stop the abuse and pollution of the land and its resources, followed by a commitment to take steps toward comprehensive remediation and conservation to restore an environment to a state of ongoing sustainability.

Our lives in Christ are renewed in a similar way. Spiritual remediation and conservation require a commitment to stop abusing and exploiting all that we are given from the hand of God. We acknowledge that all that we have and all that we are belong to him. We pause; we listen; we trust; we obey with respect to our time, relationships, finances, physical and emotional resources. The process is delicate and requires patience, but when we are committed to listening to God and cooperating with him in our daily living, we enjoy spacious ways of living and relating to God and others.

*"[W]hat we now sense as a wide-open space is a graced experience of
the real wide-open space, at whose center is the river of life, the tree of healing
for the nations, and the throne of God, with whom we will dwell forever,
face-to-face (Rev. 22:1-5)."*
—Susan P. Currie, Director, Selah Certificate Program in Spiritual Direction

THIS IS MY FATHER'S WORLD
A HYMN BY MALTBIE D. BABCOCK,1901

This is my Father's world,
And to my listening ears
All nature sings, and round me rings
The music of the spheres.
This is my Father's world:
I rest me in the thought
Of rocks and trees, of skies and seas,
His hand the wonders wrought.

This is my Father's world:
The birds their carols raise,
The morning light, the lily white,
Declare their Maker's praise.
This is my Father's world;
He shines in all that's fair;
In the rustling grass I hear Him pass,
He speaks to me everywhere

This is my Father's world:
O let me ne'er forget
That though the wrong seems oft so strong,
God is the Ruler yet.
This is my Father's world:
Why should my heart be sad?
The Lord is King: let the heavens ring!
God reigns; let earth be glad!

REFLECTION QUESTIONS

What aspects of your life promote a sense of abiding trust and reliance upon God to sustain you? What aspects of your life are "pollutants" and "invasive species"?

What kind of remediation is needed to establish a spiritually sustainable, healthy ecosystem for your soul?

How do you cooperate with or resist God's work of remediation in your life?

What is God's vision for your life? Do you have glimpses of the potential that he sees?

With whom and how can you share today an experience of open and expansive companionship?

SPIRITUAL PRACTICES

Select one of the passages of Scripture from the opening paragraphs of this chapter. Read the passage slowly three or four times and allow yourself to take in the richness of the truth it offers you.

Ponder a word or phrase that God seems to highlight for you in this moment of meditation, and allow yourself to consider how this truth speaks to your current experience.

Ask the Lord in counsel of his Spirit, what might his word be to you? Listen for his voice. If you discern something in particular, savor it in the silence. If not, resist the temptation to contrive anything, and allow yourself to stay present to God in whatever experience you have.

Read the passage again. Consider your response to God, and offer it to him in your prayer. Read the passage one last time, and then rest in his presence quietly.

A Prayer of Illumination:
Oh God, may we live openly and expansively trusting in your ways and not our own. May we live and move and have our being in you. Reclaim our lives for your glory, we pray. In Christ. Amen.

42. THE DISCIPLINE OF PLAY

RICK ANDERSON

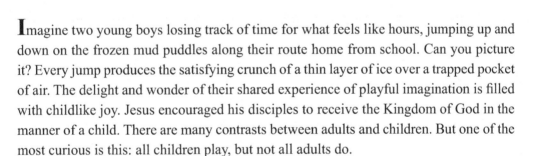

Imagine two young boys losing track of time for what feels like hours, jumping up and down on the frozen mud puddles along their route home from school. Can you picture it? Every jump produces the satisfying crunch of a thin layer of ice over a trapped pocket of air. The delight and wonder of their shared experience of playful imagination is filled with childlike joy. Jesus encouraged his disciples to receive the Kingdom of God in the manner of a child. There are many contrasts between adults and children. But one of the most curious is this: all children play, but not all adults do.

How often do you take the opportunity to play? When was the last time you lost track of time doing something that captured you with delight? Would you consider play a spiritual discipline? Perhaps that's a stretch for you. However, could a sound argument perhaps be made that play moves us into a more relaxed and joyful space internally, which enables us to be more receptive to the subtle movements of the Spirit? Often it's the things that are binding us up inside that cause the greatest resistance and rigidity in our soul. So, if play helps untangle some internal knots and makes us more receptive to God's shaping work, then maybe it is indeed a legitimate spiritual discipline – at the very least a good "pre-discipline" to the daily routines of life.

Woodworking can be a life-giving Sabbath practice for some. Regardless of what is made or how "good" it is, simply getting covered in sawdust creates an earthy connection to Jesus in a unique and tangible way. Playing with new concepts and different types of wood can be a way of forming a unique bond, knowing that Jesus himself engaged in this same activity (though without power tools). Shared activities are a way that friends experience play together. There is joy in the playfulness of a shared hobby. Perhaps you're not a woodworker, but what is it that invites you to get creative or playful?

A friend recently discovered the pottery wheel at a local retreat center and took a lesson from the resident master potter. So far the only thing he has successfully made is a mess. Even so, there's something mesmerizing about that spinning lump of clay and the complete freedom to get muddy up to his elbows. Play is not about production, it's about the release of productivity and the God-given renewal that playful delight can bring. All of us could do with some of that from time to time. How do you play?

Engaging in playfulness re-creates us – that's why it's called recreation. Similar to the discipline of rest, recreation often gets relegated to the "optional" or "must be nice to have time for that" category. This is a tragic misconception, precisely because both are divine gifts which are necessary to a full and vibrant life with God. What we forfeit when we view these renewing activities as nonessential is far more significant than we realize.

Just as his mercies are new every morning, we are in need of frequent re-creation, to be filled up with life – from the Giver of Life. So what sounds playful and joy-producing to you today? Serve yourself a healthy, guilt-free helping of it, knowing that God delights to watch his children play.

"Let the little children come to me, and do not hinder them, for the kingdom of God belongs to such as these. Truly I tell you, anyone who will not receive the kingdom of God like a little child will never enter it."
—Mark 10:14-15

"We are never more fully alive, more completely ourselves, or more deeply engrossed in anything than when we are playing."
—Charles Schaefer

HAVE THINE OWN WAY
A HYMN BY ADELAIDE A. POLLARD, 1906

Have thine own way, Lord! Have thine own way!
Thou art the potter, I am the clay.
Mold me and make me after thy will,
while I am waiting, yielded and still.

Have Thine own way, Lord! Have Thine own way!
Search me and try me, Master, today!
Whiter than snow, Lord, wash me just now,
As in Thy presence humbly I bow.

Have Thine own way, Lord! Have Thine own way!
Wounded and weary, help me, I pray!
Power, all power, surely is Thine!
Touch me and heal me, Savior divine.

Have Thine own way, Lord! Have Thine own way!
Hold o'er my being absolute sway!
Fill with Thy Spirit till all shall see
Christ only, always, living in me.

REFLECTION QUESTIONS

When was the last time you lost track of time doing something purely for the enjoyment of it?

Do you feel guilty when you take time to play? Why?

Would you consider play a legitimate spiritual discipline? If so, how?

If you were eight years old right now, what would you do for play?

When did you become persuaded that you were too old for the answer above? Perhaps that activity is worth revisiting regardless of how old you are now!

SPIRITUAL PRACTICES

Can you give yourself permission to take a break from all that is "required" of you today and just do something fun? It's good for the soul.

Invite God to join you in playful and fun activity together.

Make a list called "My Spiritual Disciplines of Play." Then begin to brainstorm the playful activities that you can get lost in (for some, when the hands are busy, the mind and spirit are freed up to be more attentive to God).

As you give yourself permission to play, be attentive to your sense of God's presence joining in with you and any notion of becoming more internally receptive to his shaping work.

A Prayer of Illumination:
Lord of all wondrous creation, invite us into playful companionship with you today, that we may know more of you through a kindred spirit of creating life and delighting in seeing it set free. In Jesus. Amen.

43. SELF-CARE

GENALIN NIERE-METCALF

A theme we too often see in our work with people in ministry is poor self-care (or the total lack thereof). In fact, when we bring up the subject of self-care it is often met with some resistance and even a sense of guilt. Some have equated self-care with being self-ish. The sacrifice of caring for oneself can easily be spiritualized because "the harvest is plentiful and the workers are few."

Yet, we can trace back to how poor self-care has impacted ministers' lives so nega-tively that it has had a ripple effect on those they served. Their lack of self-care has unnecessarily caused problems and pain to themselves and others. Sadly, some were not even aware of their negative impact on others until the problem was extensive. We are more convicted each year that self-care is an essential and responsible discipline we need to practice as people who minister to others. It is putting into practice loving others as we love ourselves (Matthew 22:39). It is honoring God and the ministry he entrusts to us.

Self-care is essential for those who minister to others because those we serve, espe-cially when they are going through difficulties, impact us. It is well known that people in care-giving roles can experience compassion fatigue, secondary trauma, and vicar-ious trauma. The impact can be slow and subtle in our lives and be undetected for a long time if we are not in tune with ourselves. Some signs and symptoms that you are lacking in self-care and developing compassion fatigue, secondary trauma, or vicarious trauma include: chronic exhaustion, sense that you can never do enough, work becoming the center of your identity (grandiosity), diminished creativity, inflexibility, guilt, fear, anger, relational problems, sleep problems, somatic complaints, lack of efficacy, helplessness, and hopelessness.

So how do we include the rhythm of self-care in our lives? When considering how you should care for yourself, take inventory of your physical, emotional, and spiritual life.

1. How am I caring for my physical self? How many hours of sleep do I get? Am I making healthy food choices? What do I do for exercise? When was my last physical check-up? Where do I want to go for a vacation? What does my body need in order to feel well and optimal?

2. How am I caring for my emotional self? How are my relationships? Am I setting healthy boundaries? What is my level of stress? Am I kind to myself? What do I need to do (or not do) to feel emotionally well and optimal?

3. How am I caring for my soul? When was the last time I had an experience of awe? Am I engaging in life-giving activities? Where do I go to still my spirit and feel close to God? Do I have a spiritual community? In what parts of my soul do I feel thirsty? What nourishment do I need for my spirit?

"Then, because so many people were coming and going that
they did not even have a chance to eat, Jesus said to them,
'Come with me by yourselves to a quiet place and get some rest.'"
—Mark 6:31

"A leader is a person who must take special responsibility for what is going on
inside him or herself, inside his or her consciousness..."
—Parker Palmer, Let Your Life Speak

SPIRIT OF THE LIVING GOD
A HYMN BY DANIEL IVERSON (b. 1890)

Spirit of the Living God
Fall afresh on me
Spirit of the Living God
Fall afresh on me
Break me, melt me,
Mold me, fill me
Spirit of the Living God
Fall afresh on me

REFLECTION QUESTIONS

What could you do differently in your life that would better care for your body?

How in tune are you with your emotions? What has been on your heart that you need to talk to God and others about?

How do you experience God in the silence? What longings do you notice in your spirit? When and where do you experience awe?

How could you make this type of physical, emotional, and spiritual inventory a regular self-care practice?

SPIRITUAL PRACTICES

Take a moment to be aware of your body, this temple that the Lord has given you. Set up an appointment for a physical checkup with your doctor, and pick one healthy change you will make as a way to glorify God with your body (1 Corinthians 6:19-20; 10:31).

Take a moment to notice how you are feeling. Allow your feelings to be a starting point of conversation with the Lord about what is on your heart (Job 7:11; Lamentations 2:19).

Find a quiet place, and take five minutes in the middle of your day to be still before the Lord and allow the nourishing silence to refresh and hold your spirit (Habakkuk 2:20; Psalm 46:10).

A Prayer of Illumination:
"Beloved, I pray that all may go well with you and that you may be in good health, as it goes well with your soul." 3 John 1:2 (ESV) *May it be so. Amen.*

44. CELEBRATION

RICK ANDERSON

Greetings, friend! What shall we celebrate today? What's the occasion? Christ is risen, you are breathing, the sun came up again this morning, you can read, it's Friday - take your pick! How could we as Christians ever truly run out of things to celebrate?

In the eyes of the world, are we celebrators or wet blankets? The empty tomb we commemorate on Easter morning means we have more to celebrate than anyone! Why then are we so often characterized as rigid and somber? We can't help but join in on Teresa of Avila's prayer, "From silly devotions and sour-faced saints, spare us, O Lord." For the fruit of the Spirit is duty, judgment, enforcement ... wait, that's not our mandate, is it? Love and Joy head that list!

Our notion of celebration may be like a bunch of stoic old biddies at a tennis match, clapping daintily: "Very good. Most enlivening." Shouldn't it be like a two-year-old who has just had the entire box of Honey Nut Cheerios dumped out in front of her wide-eyed and open-mouthed -astonishment at the sheer abundance that is ours in Christ Jesus?

Jesus tells story after story to help us grasp what the kingdom of heaven is like. Stories of a shepherd seeking and finding a lost sheep and a woman seeking and finding a lost coin both end with celebrations in heaven (what must it be like when heaven celebrates?). He's painting a picture for us.

Can we connect the dots to see that Jesus is the very arms of God reaching out to humanity, seeking and finding what belongs to God--and to see that the result of this is celebration in heaven? The final parable in the lost-and-found trifecta of Luke 15 is called the parable of the lost son, but the story is really about the Father - a Father whose first response at the homecoming of his wayward child is not anger, not disappointment, not a lecture, but a huge celebration.

Engaging in celebration is inherently communal. The Latin root means "to assemble to honor" which indicates that for celebration to occur, "some assembly is required." To celebrate. we need each other's presence. Leviticus 23 records seven feasts for the Israelites to celebrate on an annual basis. The first of these feasts is Passover, which we celebrate each time we come to the Lord's Table together. This is a time for confession, to be sure, but most certainly for celebration as well! We celebrate that our confessions are heard and our sins are forgiven because of the price Jesus paid for us at Calvary.

After a long Lenten season of waiting, the Son has risen with the sun - and because of his incredible valor and sacrifice, the veil has been torn in two, death has lost its sting, and we can be adopted as God's beloved children. Shall we party like it's 1999, or like we've got eternity in Paradise before us?

Go forth as an ambassador of joy and celebration, friend! What this lost world needs is not a measuring stick but an invitation to experience the Master's House Party.

"The kingdom of heaven may be compared to a king who gave a wedding feast for his son, and sent his servants to call those who were invited to the wedding feast ..."
—Matthew 22:2-3 (ESV)

"Christians ought to be celebrating constantly. We ought to be preoccupied with parties, banquets, feast, and merriment ... because we have been liberated from the fear of life and the fear of death. We ought to attract people to the church quite literally by the fun there is in being a Christian."
—Robert Hotchkins

AWAKE, MY SOUL, AND WITH THE SUN
A HYMN BY THOMAS KEN, 1695

Awake, my soul, and with the sun
Thy daily stage of duty run;
Shake off dull sloth, and early rise
To pay thy morning sacrifice.

Redeem thy mis-spent time that's past,
Live this day as if 'twere thy last;
T'improve thy talents take due care
'Gainst the great day thy self prepare.

Glory to God, who safe hath kept;
And hath refresh'd me while I slept;
Grant, Lord, when I from death shall wake,
I may of endless life partake.

Praise God, from whom all blessings flow;
Praise him, all creatures here below;
Praise him above, ye heav'nly host;
Praise Father, Son, and Holy Ghost.

REFLECTION QUESTIONS

Do you experience God as a task-master or a party-thrower?

Can you personally receive God's celebration of you in the words of Zephaniah 3:17 (he delights in you and rejoices over you with singing)?

Would you consider celebration to be a spiritual discipline? If so, how will you practice it?

What in your life is worth celebrating that you have perhaps overlooked?

When is your next celebration, and who will it be with?

SPIRITUAL PRACTICES

Find ways to intentionally build celebration elements into your Sabbath practices. It doesn't need to be a big production, but what could you do that would feel celebratory?

Invite God to broaden your view of celebration and joy in the kingdom of heaven. Could you dare to envision the celebration that took place in heaven on the day that you were the lost coin that was found (yes, this happened!)?

Imagine you are on the hospitality and promotion team for the wedding feast from Matthew 22. How winsome is your personal invitation to come and join the party? Are others drawn to the party because you are going?

A Prayer of Illumination:
Let joy abound and celebration ensue, Father, as we survey your goodness to us in countless ways. Comfort us in our suffering and embolden us in our celebrating. Jesus, continue to seek and reclaim what's been lost along the way - in our world, and in our own hearts. Amen.

45. ART AND SOUL

GAYLE HEASLIP

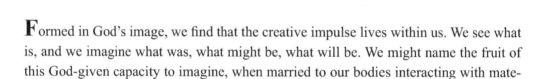

Formed in God's image, we find that the creative impulse lives within us. We see what is, and we imagine what was, what might be, what will be. We might name the fruit of this God-given capacity to imagine, when married to our bodies interacting with materials, as *art*.

While most of us are not artists by vocation, what might it mean to create art as an expression of being made in God's image? How might the practice of creating draw us to a fuller knowledge of our Lord and of ourselves? What values might God have in mind for our souls in the process of creativity as a spiritual practice?

Recently one friend confided to another that writing sometimes alarms her. What comes out in written form is not what she intends when she first sits down; there can be an edge to it, a rawness that can be disconcerting. Moving beneath the analytically trained ways in which we perceive, she finds that the process of writing often speaks a truth carefully edited from her awareness.

When we approach this revelation with a holy curiosity, it becomes material for further reflection and prayer. Sometimes it also reveals something exquisite about the Lord who is love and mercy, who is holy and just. It is not a revelation received by analysis, but by opening oneself to the Holy Other. We open up to that which is not categorical, but fluid, not containable, but expansive. We open a door to mystery, and it beckons us to something, Someone, stirring deeper waters in our souls.

Practicing art in this way, then, engenders a courageous hospitality to God's presence. We offer him room to reveal himself to us and through us, and in turn we participate in and bear witness to that revelation according to our creative preference, whether visual art, performing art, writing, or within such subtle arts as raising a family, planting a garden, or creatively providing a work atmosphere saturated with grace. Spaces for creativity abound--for co-laboring with God to fashion what reveals his nature and draws others to him.

Opening oneself up to what is beyond our control is fearsome. Art can be a daunting journey of discovery, inviting us to the edge of what is known to encounter the unknown. The desert fathers and mothers traveled to wild places to encounter God, and followers of Christ still seek wild places raw with God's presence, stripped of safety and control, open to the unexpected movement of the Spirit.

Art beckons. It enlarges our perspective, it pushes past our preconceptions, it whispers to what lies deep within our souls, to what is mystery, and we are drawn in. In the best art we encounter God. By engaging in art ourselves, we experience the God who creates and re-creates us, forming us into his likeness, to his glory and our delight. Let us respond in faith to the creative impulse within, as we offer our imagination to him and follow his lead in the creative expression that flows from our souls.

"See, I have chosen Bezalel ... and I have filled him with the Spirit of God, with skill, ability, and knowledge in all kinds of crafts—to make artistic designs...and to engage in all kinds of craftsmanship."
—Exodus 31:1-5

"Creativity activates imagination, and imagination is one of our most valuable spiritual faculties."
—Vanita Hampton Wright, The Soul Tells a Story

HOW GREAT THOU ART!
A HYMN BY STUART K. HINE, 1885

O Lord my God, When I, in awesome wonder
Consider all the worlds Thy Hands have made;
I see the stars, I hear the rolling thunder,
Thy power throughout the universe displayed.

Chorus:
Then sings my soul, My Saviour God, to Thee,
How great Thou art, How great Thou art!
Then sings my soul, My Saviour God, to Thee,
How great Thou art, How great Thou art!

When through the woods and forest glades I wander,
And hear the birds sing sweetly in the trees.
When I look down from lofty mountain grandeur
And see the brook, and feel the gentle breeze,

And when I think, that God, His Son not sparing,
Sent Him to die, I scarce can take it in;
That on the Cross, my burden gladly bearing,
He bled and died to take away my sin.

When Christ shall come, with shout of acclamation,
And take me home, what joy shall fill my heart.
Then I shall bow, in humble adoration,
And then proclaim: "My God, how great Thou art!"

REFLECTION QUESTIONS

What moves you or captures your attention through the creative expression of others? The next time you watch a thoughtful movie, go to a musical performance, play, or dance, or visit a museum, reflect on the internal experience. What stood out to you? What might the Lord be drawing your attention to? How might you respond to any awareness that arises?

How are your life and those around you enriched by creativity? Consider the ways in which creativity is already expressed in your life. How do you arrange your environment to be more pleasing, plan a meal that stirs the senses, play with children, give creative expression to your soul?

SPIRITUAL PRACTICES

If there is a creative expression you are already drawn to or experienced in, consider prayerfully opening yourself to the Lord through practicing it on a regular basis for a month. Notice how this practice flows into other areas of your life with God and others.

Practice *visio divina.* Set apart 15-30 minutes to sit before a work of art that "speaks" to you. Invite the Lord's presence. Let your eyes take in the overall composition, then notice what draws your attention. Linger here to become aware of what is stirred within you. Form a prayer to the Lord around your awareness.

Without editing the expression, respond creatively to the beauty of creation or a passage of Scripture. Or draw the story of your journey with Christ or how you imagine this point in your journey with him.

A Prayer of Illumination:
My Lord, Creator of all that exists and the One who held me in Your imagination, choosing me to be Your own before You formed the earth, grant me through a sanctified imagination the freedom to practice creative expression under Your inspiration. In this way, draw me deeper into the glorious mystery of Yourself, and may this practice of creativity also serve to draw others to You. Amen.

46. BODY AND SOUL

MEAH HEARINGTON ARAKAKI

---◆---

Have you ever been frustrated with your body? Have there been times when it does not work the way you would like? What about those extra pounds that don't seem to ever disappear? Or that part of your physical appearance that you would like to change? All of us at some point have been frustrated with this earthly form that we've been given. But have you ever wondered what connection it has with your soul? Do your body and its health affect your spiritual life? the vitality of your soul?

1 Corinthians 3:16 in *The Message* states, "You realize, don't you, that you are the temple of God, and God himself is present in you? No one will get by with vandalizing God's temple, you can be sure of that. God's temple is sacred—and you, remember, are the temple." In this passage, Paul is primarily talking about sexual immorality; however, the message of our bodies being the temple of God is clear: "and you, remember, are the temple." We, our souls and bodies, house the Spirit of God. It is where he dwells. The soul is your essence: body, mind, and spirit.

What practical implications does this have on our spiritual disciplines? What does it mean to care for this body that we have been given, the place where God dwells? We often hear of soul care; does care of one's body have any relation to caring for our souls?

Gerald May, in *Care of Mind, Care of Spirit*, writes, "Humans are physical beings. We are incarnated. The life of our bodies and minds is both an expression of and prerequisite for our growth as souls." We humans are both spirit beings and physical beings. We cannot deny, or ignore, either part of our selves. If we fail to be integrated in spiritual disciplines of both body and soul, we lack a piece of God's best for us in this world.

Many books on spiritual disciplines cover in great depth the importance of prayer, meditation, silence, and so on. These disciplines are central to the life of a believer and are not to be ignored. However, there seems to be a lack of awareness about what it means to be a spiritual being within a body. How do we craft a spiritual discipline of physical wellness for the sake of our souls?

Curt Thompson, in *Anatomy of the Soul*, writes, "We don't earn brownie points with God for engaging in spiritual disciplines. They're valuable because they line us up to be more available to hear the Spirit of God when he speaks. They create space within us for God to work." What would it look like for you to have eating practices that create a healthy body that makes space for God? What would it look like for you to engage in sleeping or exercise patterns that help your body to feel alert and alive to the activity of God in your soul?

We worship God with our whole selves: body, mind, heart, and spirit. Consider the connection between your physical state and the state of your soul. Your soul is affected when your body is tired, exhausted, and haggard. But when you nourish your body well, you are also caring for your soul.

"So here's what I want you to do, God helping you: Take your everyday, ordinary life—your sleeping, eating, going-to-work, and walking-around life—and place it before God as an offering."
—Romans 12: 1 (The Message)

"To experience a little hunger now and then can be a beautiful reminder of the deeper hunger of our souls."
—Gerald May

BREATHE ON ME, BREATH OF GOD
A HYMN BY EDWIN HATCH, 1878

Breathe on me, Breath of God,
fill me with life anew,
that I may love what thou dost love,
and do what thou wouldst do.

Breathe on me, Breath of God,
until my heart is pure,
until with thee I will one will,
to do and to endure.

Breathe on me, Breath of God,
till I am wholly thine,
till all this earthly part of me
glows with thy fire divine.

Breathe on me, Breath of God,
so shall I never die,
but live with thee the perfect life
of thine eternity.

REFLECTION QUESTIONS

What would it look like to engage in a spiritual discipline that focuses on the care of your body? (Examples: Regular sleep/wake times, a prayer inviting God to join you as you eat, increasing healthy foods that you put in your body, regular movement/exercise.)

What does it look like for you to be a steward of the body that God has given to you?

In what ways do you nurture and nourish your body and soul together?

Often your body gives you indicators about the state of your overall being. What is your body telling you about the state of your soul?

SPIRITUAL PRACTICES

Be attentive to your body and your physical state. Take time to name your physical state of being on a daily basis for the next week. Journal about your awareness, and reflect on it with God.

Spend time in prayer with God, reflecting on your current practices of physical care, focusing on your awareness of health and vitality, and noting any new practice that God is inviting you into.

Invite God into your time of exercise, sleep, or eating. Ask him to be present with you in those particular places and times of engaging in the care of your body and soul.

A Prayer of Illumination:
Father, you created me with a body and a soul. Please reveal to me how to lean into my fullness, and how to make space for you in all areas of my life. I offer to you, O Lord, myself, my soul and body, to be a living sacrifice, through Jesus Christ, my Lord. Amen.

SERVICE

47. REFORMATION OF THE SOUL

STEPHEN A. MACCHIA

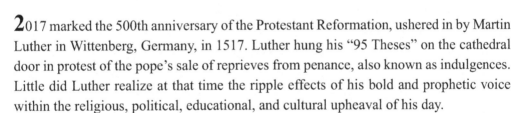

2017 marked the 500th anniversary of the Protestant Reformation, ushered in by Martin Luther in Wittenberg, Germany, in 1517. Luther hung his "95 Theses" on the cathedral door in protest of the pope's sale of reprieves from penance, also known as indulgences. Little did Luther realize at that time the ripple effects of his bold and prophetic voice within the religious, political, educational, and cultural upheaval of his day.

At Leadership Transformations we gladly recognize the historical call to purify the church and uphold the Bible as our sole authority of spiritual guidance and hope. We also commemorate the other main themes of the Reformation, which have been embedded in our movement over the past 500 years. These include the Five Solas--Sola Gratia: Grace Alone; Sola Fide: Faith Alone; Sola Scriptura: Scripture Alone; Solus Christus: Christ Alone; and Soli Deo Gloria: Glory to God Alone--as well as other important themes such as priesthood of all believers, marriage as a means of holiness, etc.

From our vantage point, however, the "reformation of the soul" is to be our number one priority. As such, the soul's reformation does not occur due to religious, political, educational,or cultural means. No, the soul is re-formed when it realizes how de-formed it can become when such external influences place upon it unhealthy demands and pull us away from the pursuit of godliness. We need to acknowledge how our affections for everything but God keep us from abiding in and with God. Only then will the soul be reformed.

Our ministry team leaders are taking this seriously. We have chosen to prioritize the ongoing reformation of our souls in this way: 1. *Daily prayer:* spacious time alone with God in the Word, in prayer, and in personal reflection. 2. *Weekly Sabbath:* 24 hours per week of life-giving rest for body, mind, and soul. 3. *Monthly direction:* sitting with a spiritual director for listening, guidance, and prayerful reflection. 4. *Quarterly retreats:* full days set apart for unhurried, unhindered, uncluttered refreshment of body, mind, and soul. 5. *Annual retreats:* extended days of contemplative soul care AND ministry team retreats for celebration of our relationships and our shared ministry.

We know that we must place these large rocks in our planning and scheduling jar first, or the sand pebbles of "lesser things" will fill up all the space. We also know that these all-important practices will undoubtedly lead to the reformation of the soul of our organization and the soul of each person within our ministry family.

Consider today how best to lean into the reformation of your own soul. What is the current state of your soul? Who or what is keeping your soul from being properly nurtured? What are the spiritual practices that will enhance your intimacy with God: Father, Son, and Holy Spirit? With whom will you share these priorities in community?

"Truly my soul finds rest in God; my salvation comes from him. Truly he is my rock and my salvation; he is my fortress, I will never be shaken."
—Psalm 62:1, 2

"Whatever your heart clings to and confides in, that is really your God...the God of this world is riches, pleasure and pride."
—Martin Luther

A MIGHTY FORTRESS
A HYMN BY MARTIN LUTHER, 1529

A mighty fortress is our God,
a bulwark never failing;
our helper he, amid the flood
of mortal ills prevailing.
For still our ancient foe
doth seek to work us woe;
his craft and power are great,
and armed with cruel hate,
on earth is not his equal.

Did we in our own strength confide,
our striving would be losing,
were not the right Man on our side,
the Man of God's own choosing.
Dost ask who that may be?
Christ Jesus, it is he;
Lord Sabaoth his name,
from age to age the same;
and he must win the battle.

And tho this world, with devils filled,
should threaten to undo us,
we will not fear, for God has willed
his truth to triumph through us.
The prince of darkness grim,
we tremble not for him;
his rage we can endure,
for lo! his doom is sure;
one little word shall fell him.

That Word above all earthly powers,
no thanks to them, abideth;
the Spirit and the gifts are ours
through him who with us sideth.
Let goods and kindred go,
this mortal life also;
the body they may kill:
God's truth abideth still;
his kingdom is forever!

REFLECTION QUESTIONS

"A Mighty Fortress" is based on Psalm 46. Meditate on that great psalm, focusing on verse 10, "Be still and know that I am God." In what ways is stillness a part of your spiritual practices?

What would a reformed soul look like for you today and in the coming months? What spiritual practices would you like to pursue which will enhance your intimacy with God?

Who is your *anam cara* (soul friend), and how would you like to deepen that relationship?

What changes would your spiritual community need to consider in order to experience reformation?

SPIRITUAL PRACTICES

Practice *Examen* today by reflecting on the following:

Review: look back and recall the blessings of the past day/week/year

Thank: give thanks to God for the joy of your with-God life (notice especially your feelings/affect)

Confess: voice to God the ways you have erred from his will and disobeyed his Word
Pray: ask God for his forgiveness, grace, love, and mercy to renew your soul once more
Preview: look ahead and prepare your heart for the coming day/week/year (journal your desires)

A Prayer of Illumination:
Thank you, Lord God Almighty, for always being my refuge and my strength, my ever-present help in times of trouble, and my hope in times of uncertainty. I praise you for being ever-present, all-knowing, and unfailing love. I trust you today as I'm still before you, knowing you are my God and I am your child forever. Amen.

48. VOCATION

JEREMY STEFANO

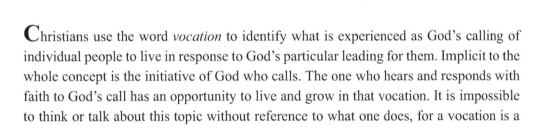

Christians use the word *vocation* to identify what is experienced as God's calling of individual people to live in response to God's particular leading for them. Implicit to the whole concept is the initiative of God who calls. The one who hears and responds with faith to God's call has an opportunity to live and grow in that vocation. It is impossible to think or talk about this topic without reference to what one does, for a vocation is a summons to work in the will of God. Jesus drew attention to his Father's ongoing works and to the fact that he too must work (John 5:17). A vocation is the calling to do one's share in the works of God.

The first vocation mentioned in the Bible involved doing the work of park rangers, tending to animals and beautiful landscapes. From there the work expanded to ship building and masonry, artistry and accounting, management of the home, administration of the homeland. Added to this is the mission of Messiah, proclaiming the good news of God's kingdom to captives, and reversing the effects of sin and its accompanying injustice on the earth. As God calls people, he equips them for their vocation with talents, inclinations, and spiritual empowerment. Then God calls out from us what he has seeded into us. Living in one's calling will involve using the gifts God has given.

It can be hard to identify what one's vocation truly is. Our first priority in participating with God in his work is to stay yoked with Jesus. Without Jesus nothing lasting or substantial gets done. Mother Teresa was once approached by a sincere young man desiring to serve with her. He expressed how attracted he was to the work of serving lepers. Discerning in him an attachment to the work that detracted from the foundational vocation, she responded, "Our vocation consists in belonging to Jesus." There is always the temptation to put avocation--even noble ones--first.

My vocation is not for me; it is for others. If I set out to attain something exclusively for myself with the gifts God has given me, it is a dismal business. What God has called and gifted me to be and to do is for the blessing and benefit of others. Responding to God's call and claim on one's life will require that what God has given to a person will be used in such a way that the good fruits of that vocation will be lavished on others. While we do derive joy from the satisfaction of our labor, God has given us to be stewards, to share what we each received for the common good.

These three facets can help in discerning and staying attuned to our true vocation: I am called to belong to Jesus and to abide in him; God's call on my life involves using gifts he has given to me; and obedience to my vocation will bring blessing to others.

"Our vocation consists in belonging to Jesus. Our work is nothing but a means to express our love for him. That is why the work itself is not [most] important. What is important is for you to belong to Jesus."
—Mother Teresa

"There is no deeper meaning in life than to discover and live out your calling... Your calling is deeper than your job, your career, and all your benchmarks of success. It is never too late to discover your calling."
—Os Guinness

DRAW THOU MY SOUL, O CHRIST
A HYMN BY LUCY LARCOM, 1892

Draw Thou my soul, O Christ, closer to Thine;
Breathe into every wish Thy will divine!
Raise my low self above, won by Thy boundless love;
Ever, O Christ, through mine, let Thy life shine.

Lead forth my soul, O Christ, one with Thine own,
Joyful to follow Thee through paths unknown!
In Thee my strength renew; give me my work to do!
Through me Thy truth be shown, Thy love made known.

Not for myself alone may my prayer be;
Lift Thou Thy world, O Christ, closer to thee!
Cleanse it from guilt and wrong; teach it salvation's song,
Till earth, as heaven, fulfill God's holy will.

REFLECTION QUESTIONS

How does belonging to Jesus grace the way you fulfill your vocation?

Is there a way you are tempted to use your gifts to serve yourself rather than stewarding them for the good of others?

What benefits and satisfaction do you enjoy in responding to God's call?

Who are the beneficiaries of your faithfulness in vocation?

SPIRITUAL PRACTICES

Remember those who helped identify or validate your vocation.

Make a time to sit with a friend and exchange what encourages or blesses each of you about who the other is, and about what each of you is called to do.

Notice what feels like clutter in your life that inhibits faithfulness in your vocation.

Find an opportunity to affirm someone who you discern is living freely in their vocation, or to encourage someone who perhaps is struggling to do so.

A Prayer of Illumination:
You loved me. You gifted me. You called me, Father.
May I be grounded in your love, sharing generously, and doing all you ask of me. Amen.

49. PERSECUTION

JEREMY STEFANO

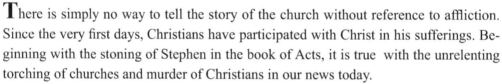

There is simply no way to tell the story of the church without reference to affliction. Since the very first days, Christians have participated with Christ in his sufferings. Beginning with the stoning of Stephen in the book of Acts, it is true with the unrelenting torching of churches and murder of Christians in our news today.

The plight of persecuted Christians can be surveyed by accounts of diverse people and circumstances such as Perpetua and Felicity from North Africa, who were imprisoned in Rome and martyred in 203; Jan Hus, who was burned at the stake in 1415 for teaching theological views that contradicted Roman Catholic thought; John Bunyan, repeatedly arrested and imprisoned for much of the 1660s and 1670s for unauthorized preaching in his native England; Maximilian Kolbe, a Franciscan priest who offered to die in place of another prisoner, selected for death by starvation in Auschwitz in 1941; Oscar Romero, Archbishop of San Salvador, assassinated in 1980 because of his unyielding preference for the poor in his country and his criticism of the oppressive power of the rich.

Our own time is not without its martyrs, whose stories can be recounted in numbers. The Center for the Study of Global Christianity estimates that 1 million Christians were martyred in the first 10 years of this century. The words Peter wrote before he was martyred for his faith in Jesus are true still today: "Dear friends, do not be surprised at the fiery ordeal that has come on you to test you, as though something strange were happening to you. But rejoice inasmuch as you participate in the sufferings of Christ, so that you may be overjoyed when his glory is revealed." 1 Peter 4:12-13

In his book *100 Prison Meditations*, Richard Wurmbrand (1909-2001), a Romanian pastor imprisoned and tortured repeatedly under Communism, recalls this story: "A sufferer once came to a pastor and asked him many questions. The pastor answered, 'Kneel here in church and ask Jesus for the answers.' The man replied, 'Do you really think I will hear a voice from heaven?' 'No,' said the pastor, 'but by keeping quiet in prayer for several hours before God, you will realize that you can go along without answers to all your problems. You do not need more than his peace, which passes all understanding.'" There is nothing easy in these words, and no possibility of anything trite in the answer, given that these are the words of one who spent fourteen years in prison, three of them in solitary confinement.

While we are all called upon to suffer in this life in some way, may we be faithful to remember those who suffer for our shared faith and hope in Christ, as if we were "together with them in prison." Hebrews 13:3

"Reading the Bible in a solitary cell, from memory, I am struck by the extent to which suffering pervades it… Why do even Christians have to suffer? Faith in God is the sole answer to the mystery of evil."
—Richard Wurmbrand, 100 Prison Meditations

"The most common request of persecuted Christians is 'PRAY FOR US.'"
—Voice of the Martyrs website

FAITH OF OUR FATHERS
A HYMN BY REV. F. W. FABER,(1849

Faith of our fathers, living still
In spite of dungeon, fire and sword
O how our hearts beat high with joy
Whene'er we hear that glorious word!
Faith of our fathers! Holy faith!
We will be true to thee till death.

Our mothers chained in prisons dark
Were still in heart and conscience free
How sweet would be their children's fate
If they, like them, could die for Thee!
Faith of our mothers! Holy faith!
We will be true to thee till death.

Faith of our fathers we will love
Both friend and foe in all our strife
And preach thee too as love knows how
By kindly words and virtuous life!
Faith of our fathers! Holy faith!
We will be true to thee till death.

REFLECTION QUESTIONS

What arises in my heart when I hear of Christians who are being persecuted today?

Can I live without an answer to vexing, pressing questions?

Why do Christians have to suffer?

Is there something I can do to call attention and offer comfort to our afflicted sisters and brothers in Christ?

SPIRITUAL PRACTICES

Remember those who are oppressed, homeless, or in prison for their witness to Jesus Christ.

Pray for the persecuted church.

Learn about a country where persecution of Christians is a present threat.

Read accounts of believers who have endured suffering and hardship for their faith in the Lord.

A Prayer of Illumination:
Heavenly Father, look upon your holy people who are suffering. You will reward their faith in the life to come; comfort them now in sorrow and affliction. They are the bold meek of the earth, the suffering hopeful. Have mercy on them, O Lord. Have mercy. In the Name of Christ Jesus. Amen.

50. RECEPTIVITY

RICK ANDERSON

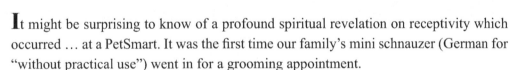

It might be surprising to know of a profound spiritual revelation on receptivity which occurred … at a PetSmart. It was the first time our family's mini schnauzer (German for "without practical use") went in for a grooming appointment.

We were immediately taken aback by the scope of the whole operation: multiple groomers, each with their own station equipped with grooming table, water, shampoos, and a variety of shearing accessories – and all of this encased in a glass-walled room like a high-tech scientific laboratory. What struck us next was the variety of dogs in size, shape, and temperament on the tables. Some hyper, some fearful, some yelping, and others quiet and still as the groomers worked their magic. It was as if God whispered in that moment, "This is a picture of your ongoing spiritual formation. I am the Groomer and you are the dog."

From the dog groomer's perspective, this process is pretty straightforward: "I know what I'm doing. I'm very good at this. Some dogs are easier to work with than others. If the dog is receptive to what I'm trying to do, it goes a lot better. If not, it just takes longer. Regardless, I will shape this scruffy pooch into what it's supposed to look like. Nothing is more gratifying than the transformation from mangy to immaculate. It's what I do." There's not much the dog can do to speed up the process, but certainly there are things the dog can do to slow it down. Pull at the leash, bark, jump around, spill things, cower and quiver in confusion – or simply hold still while the work is done.

The prospect of being shaped into the image of Christ is a somewhat overwhelming and intimidating thought to consider. But emulating a dog who has learned to hold still while the Master does his work? That's more our speed! God knows that well, and I'm grateful for the gift of this silly memory that stays with me to this day. He knows each of us intimately and shapes us uniquely. He knows how much we need and how much we can handle. And one thing is clear: Any transformation is his to claim.

What a liberating thought, that we are shaped not by our own efforts but by the Spirit's handiwork! And the more receptive we are to the process, the more opportunity we have to work with God rather than against him.

How receptive are you to God's shaping work in you? Is there any consolation in acknowledging that God is shaping you very intentionally – even in the things that are hard, scary, confusing, and painful? Is there comfort in remembering his constant presence throughout the process and the purposefulness of his workmanship?

Whether you aspire to be a compliant dog or just a cooperative disciple, both images invite humility – a good place to start in becoming more receptive to God.

"In all my prayers for all of you, I always pray with joy because of your partnership in the gospel from the first day until now, being confident of this, that he who began a good work in you will carry it on to completion until the day of Christ Jesus."
—Philippians 1:4-6

"God is always coming to you in the sacrament of the present moment. Meet and receive him there with gratitude."
—Evelyn Underhill

DAY BY DAY
A HYMN BY CAROLINA SANDELL, 1865

Day by day and with each passing moment,
Strength I find to meet my trials here;
Trusting in my Father's wise bestowment,
I've no cause for worry or for fear.
He whose heart is kind beyond all measure
Gives unto each day what He deems best--
Lovingly, its part of pain and pleasure,
Mingling toil with peace and rest.

Ev'ry day the Lord Himself is near me
With a special mercy for each hour;
All my cares He fain would bear and cheer me,
He whose name is Counselor and Pow'r.
The protection of His child and treasure
Is a charge that on Himself He laid;
"As thy days, thy strength shall be in measure,"
This the pledge to me He made.

Help me then in every tribulation
So to trust Thy promises, O Lord,
That I lose not faith's sweet consolation
Offered me within Thy holy Word.
Help me, Lord, when toil and trouble meeting,
E'er to take, as from a father's hand,
One by one, the days, the moments fleeting,
Till I reach the promised land.

REFLECTION QUESTIONS

Read the Parable of the Sower from Luke 8:4-8. This parable is all about receptivity!

As you read this familiar passage, what word or phrase stands out to you today?

In what ways can you identify each of the types of soil Jesus mentions in your own heart?

Why do you think Jesus chose the imagery of seeds and soil to illustrate receptivity? Is there a small step you could take today to increase your receptivity to God and his shaping work?

SPIRITUAL PRACTICES

Here are a few practices that can put us in a receptive posture. (A brief guide to each of these practices and many more is available at wwwSpiritualFormationStore.com.):

Receive a short passage of Scripture as a gift just for you today through Lectio Divina (sacred reading).

Receive what God has to say to you today through Listening Prayer.

Receive insight and gratitude through the practice of Daily Examen.

Receive and hold your own story through Reflective Journaling.

A Prayer of Illumination:
Heavenly Father, thank you for your patient, skillful, and deliberate shaping work. May we entrust ourselves to you, knowing that the process is not finished and you will be faithful to complete it according to your will. Quiet our hearts, and give us the grace and courage to hold still while you work. Amen.

51. THE DISCIPLINE OF GENEROSITY

DIANA CURREN BENNETT

◆

What comes to mind when you hear "God loves a cheerful giver"? Perhaps the vision of a white- knuckled child holding his/her precious coins of hard-earned allowance fills your mind and brings memories of modeling generosity with children. Along with being cheerful, God invites us to be generous. Usually money comes to mind. And it is important to give cheerfully and generously back to God for his purposes and to those who are in need. After all, all of what we consider "our own" has graciously been entrusted to us by a generous God and belongs fully to him.

In what ways has God been generous with us? What does it look like for us to be generous in response to God's generosity? God gives us the most perfect example of generosity: his grace. He sent his Son, whose life bought us salvation. We can never out-give God, and he has lavished his unending, amazing grace on us…his children.

"Remember this: Whoever sows sparingly will also reap sparingly, and whoever sows generously will also reap generously. Each man should give what he has decided in his heart to give, not reluctantly or under compulsion, for God loves a cheerful giver. And God is able to make all grace abound to you, so that in all things at all times, having all that you need, you will abound in every good work…You will be made rich in every way so that you can be generous on every occasion, and through us your generosity will result in thanksgiving to God." 2 Corinthians 9:6-8, 11

For us, generosity looks like freely giving to others, and doing so with grace-filled attitudes and actions. Remember, every gift we have originates from God. To be generous is to offer what we have, whether in moderation or in abundance, to those in need. Being generous does not always depend on finances. We show generosity by using our various giftedness: generosity with on-going forgiveness; generosity with our love, attention and compassion; generosity with moments of attentive listening; and generosity with whatever it takes to help another discover not only the love of God, but personal encouragement in the transformational experience toward Christlikeness.

Let us pray that God will remind us of the many ways he has been generous to us. Let us ask him for a generous spirit, a release of what we think we deserve to cling to, and a mind-set of release in order to assist those in need. History confirms that generosity has a rippling effect. The young pastor who once received financial help now leads many to new life in Christ. The church and leaders that once needed care now mentor others with life-giving spiritual formation. And the mission that depends on donations brings the gospel to a culture without hope. We give out of our abundance with a posture of thankfulness and for the glory of God. Yes, God smiles on the cheerful and generous heart!

"Good will come to him who is generous and lends freely..."
—Psalm 112:5a

"But since you excel in everything—in faith, in speech, in knowledge,
in complete earnestness and in the love we have kindled in you[a]
—see that you also excel in this grace of giving."
—2 Corinthians 8:7

Clearly, giving generously releases resources. And while the resources liberated through acts of generosity are a blessing, they are literally a 'by-product' of the transformational power of generosity within the giver's heart. For "where your treasure is, there your heart will be also(Matthew 6:21).

MAKE ME A BLESSING
A HYMN BY IRA B. WILSON, 1880-1950

Out in the highways and byways of life,
Many are weary and sad;
Carry the sunshine where darkness is rife,
Making the sorrowing glad.

Tell the sweet story of Christ and His love,
Tell of His power to forgive;
Others will trust Him if only you prove
True, every moment you live. (Refrain)

Give as 'twas given to you in your need,
Love as the Master loved you;
Be to the helpless a helper indeed,
Unto your mission be true. (Refrain)

Refrain: Make me a blessing, Make me a blessing;
Out of my life may Jesus shine.
Make me a blessing, O Savior, I pray
Make me a blessing to someone today!

REFLECTION QUESTIONS

In your journal, list the many ways God has been generous to you. Make a list of your generous responses to God's gifts to you. Be thankful!

Reflect on how "cheerful" and "generous" you are with your material goods. Prayerfully consider your time and involvement with certain people or organizations.

Ask the Lord to open your eyes to specific giving opportunities. This might be a stretch of your giving in the past. It might also require some quality time you have been protecting.

SPIRITUAL PRACTICES

Start each morning in prayer, asking God to show you where you might be generous during the day. Practice the prayer of examen at night, reflecting on opportunities you responded or did not respond to.

Think of a friend, neighbor, or community need. Ask God what his invitation to you might be concerning your generosity and their situation.

Ask God to show you a specific need that you are in a position to help meet with money or time (perhaps helping a student or organization struggling with tuition or meeting a budget). Then: Act!

A Prayer of Illumination:
Father in heaven, we stand in awe of your unfathomable extravagance of generosity through your Son Jesus, who bought our salvation. Thank you for uncountable gifts of grace, talents, and treasures. We pray for receptive, generous hearts as you invite us to share what you so lavishly lend to us for the furthering of your kingdom. And for this we give thanks in your Holy Name, Father, Son, and Holy Spirit. Amen.

52. A LIFE OF WORSHIP

TOM GRIFFITH

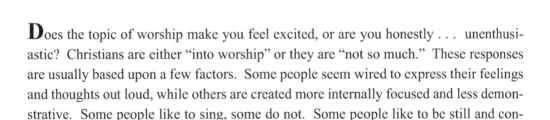

Does the topic of worship make you feel excited, or are you honestly . . . unenthusiastic? Christians are either "into worship" or they are "not so much." These responses are usually based upon a few factors. Some people seem wired to express their feelings and thoughts out loud, while others are created more internally focused and less demonstrative. Some people like to sing, some do not. Some people like to be still and contemplative, others are action-oriented. Most people's response to the topic of worship is based upon a mixture of their personality and their corporate experiences of worship.

There is a lot of overt and covert judgment in the body of Christ around the issue of worship styles. This should not be. We must strengthen our understanding of worship and help one another "enter in" more deeply. Worship is an expression of God's worth – it is a declaration that God is worthy of all our attention and praise ... but there is more. It is an expression of our covenant relationship with him – an expression of identity, love and oneness. It's an encounter with the Creator and King of everything.

There is a protocol for having audience with any king. You don't barge into a throne room--you enter appropriately. Psalm 100:4 describes a process and progression in worship. We enter with thanks and praise. Thanks may be silent or whispered, but praise is a declaration. When thanks is expressed aloud, it is praise. Praise may also declare who God is and/or what he has done. Thanks and praise lift our attention from ourselves toward God. Speaking it out loud is a function of our rightful place in his created order. He who spoke creation into being placed humans as image bearers over his creation. When we speak truth about God over his creation, we are bearing his image. This affects the spiritual atmosphere within us and around us – it declares his Lordship.

Praise gives way to a more intimate expression of worship. It speaks *to* God, not just *about* him. This is a personal declaration of what God means to us, and of our devotion to him. It is a cherished, "face-to-face" expression of loving commitment. It moves from declaring the power and authority of our covenant in Christ to an intimate expression of mutual identity. "I am my Beloved's and He is mine" (Song of Songs 6:3). We are declaring that his will is ours, that we receive and represent his name, that we are in him and he is in us (John 17:20-23).

This intimacy often takes us yet further, to stillness and silence. We are awed in his presence; at peace, content, or possibly overwhelmed. We are silenced before him. It is often in this stage of silent oneness that God speaks with his gentle whisper to our soul. We hear the "Word of the Lord" in a fresh, powerful, and directive way.

As awesome and valuable as this entire progression is thus far, it is still not complete. The voice of the Lord leads us into another important step: covenant obedience. Worship is ultimately an expression of covenant obedience to God's intimate leading. This is the life of Jesus. This releases greater expressions and experiences of oneness, and more covenant obedience. This becomes our lifestyle of worship (Romans 12:1-2).

"Worship is the missing jewel in modern evangelicalism."
—A.W. Tozer

*"When God's people begin to praise and worship Him using
the Biblical methods He gives, the Power of His presence comes among
His people in an even greater measure."*
—Graham Truscott

A THOUSAND ORACLES DIVINE
A HYMN BY CHARLES WESLEY, 1767

A thousand oracles divine
Their common beams unite,
That sinners may with angels join
To worship God aright.

Triumphant host! They never cease
To laud and magnify
The Triune God of holiness,
Whose glory fills the sky.

By faith the upper choir we meet,
And challenge them to sing
Jehovah on his shining seat,
Our Maker and our King.

But God made flesh is wholly ours,
And asks our nobler strain;
The Father of celestial powers,
The friend of earth born man!

REFLECTION QUESTIONS

Does expressing worship seem to come easily for you, or is it difficult? Why?

Do you think you would benefit from increasing your capacity to be with and worship God? What kind of difference might it make?

Are you aware of anything hindering your worship that you can address – any barriers to remove?

If you sense God's prompting to build more intentional worship into your life, what are some steps you might take? Are you ready to make a simple executable plan to grow in worship?

SPIRITUAL PRACTICES

Spend some time silently (or in writing) expressing thanks to God for specific things he has done.

Spend some time alone expressing praise and thanks out loud – declare who he is and what he has done, is doing and will do.

Quiet your soul (Psalm 131:2), and simply be still with God … no questions, requests or intercession – just be with him.

If you sense God may be saying anything to you, jot it down and return to being still.

A Prayer of Illumination:
Father, please give me the patience and perseverance to come closer and still my soul before You. Your presence and Your Word are my life and direction. In Jesus. Amen.

SEASONS

53. THE CHURCH YEAR

SUSAN PORTERFIELD CURRIE

"**A**hhh, Spring!… a word, a color, a scent makes us immediately present to the season and all that it invites. We smell a blossoming apple tree and we haul out the barbeque grill; we feel the springy freshly mown lawn beneath our feet and we head to the baseball park. Seasons, marking time with their ever-returning familiarity, evoke feeling and shape action that root us in a place and a history and into the rhythmic order of the creation.

So it is with the Church Year. We mark seasons, and events, that ground us in the life of Jesus among us, and in the grand story of redemption. And in the process, we are shaped into that story, into his image, and prepared for his return.

The Church Year is centered around the great feasts representing the central events of Jesus' life—Christmas, Easter, and Pentecost. And each feast is surrounded by a season, with its own biblical focus and its own spiritual work. Each is captured by a particular tone, even a particular color, helping us to access the story and the spiritual work with our senses, much as spring green calls us out for a walk, or autumn color prompts us to order wood for the fireplace.

In summary: This sin-soaked world waits, in hope, for the Savior to come (Advent, purple or deep royal blue); we celebrate his birth (Christmas) for 12 days, and then his appearing (Epiphany) to the wise men and later to his followers as he revealed his glory among them. But Jesus came with a mission, and so we turn with him to the cross, journeying the 40 days of Lent (based on Jesus' 40-day wilderness sojourn and the Israelites' 40-year exodus from slavery). It is a somber time (penitential purple), when we strip outwardly of encumbrances in order to strip inwardly of the sin that so easily entangles. Holy Week, and we wait at the cross, and the tomb; then Easter morn—Alleluia! Christ is Risen! All our senses celebrate; trumpet song, lily scent, the white of purity! It is our greatest celebration, lasting 40 days to Jesus' Ascension, then 10 more days until Pentecost (symbolized by the color red for flames of fire), when the Holy Spirit comes to indwell his Church. This leads us into 'Ordinary Time,' when the Spirit-filled Church grows in kingdom life and fruitfulness (green, the color of life), until we reach the last Sunday of the Church Year—Christ the King Sunday, acknowledging Jesus on the throne and awaiting his return. And then we once again lean into that return, with Advent.

Keeping the Church Year shapes us for eternity in the New Creation. We pray its movements and learn its rhythms—how to resist temptation, how to die to sin, how to nurture and celebrate kingdom-fruitful life, how to wait in hope. Our sadness, our hurt, our longing, our rejoicing—all find their place in the worship of the church through the cycle of time. Practicing thus, year in and year out, we become people who live into the fullness of Jesus' return, into the fullness of eternal life.

The Lord said to Moses, "Speak to the Israelites and say to them: '
These are my appointed festivals, the appointed festivals of the Lord,
which you are to proclaim as sacred assemblies . . . This is to be a lasting ordinance
for the generations to come, wherever you live.'"
—Leviticus 23:1-2, 14

"We want to inhabit the still-unfolding Story of God and have it inhabit
and change us. And this is exactly what the ancient liturgical habit of living
the Christian Year helps us to do."
—Bobby Gross, Living the Christian Year: Time to Inhabit the Story of God

AT THE NAME OF JESUS
A HYMN BY CAROLINE M. NOEL (1870) (BASED ON PHILIPPIANS 2)

At the Name of Jesus, every knee shall bow,
Every tongue confess Him King of glory now;
'Tis the Father's pleasure we should call Him Lord,
Who from the beginning was the mighty Word.

Humbled for a season, to receive a name
From the lips of sinners unto whom He came,
Faithfully He bore it, spotless to the last,
Brought it back victorious when from death He passed.

Bore it up triumphant with its human light,
Through all ranks of creatures, to the central height,
To the throne of Godhead, to the Father's breast;
Filled it with the glory of that perfect rest.

Brothers, this Lord Jesus shall return again,
With His Father's glory, with His angel train;
For all wreaths of empire meet upon His brow,
And our hearts confess Him King of glory now.

REFLECTION QUESTIONS

As you move through nature's seasons, how do they affect your body? your soul? What might it look like to let the Church Year give home to and shape the rhythms of your body and soul?

What one-word prayer might capture each season? How might you pray it with your posture?

If you're in church leadership, what would it look like for your congregation's common worship to journey through the life of Jesus and the seasons of the spiritual life? How might you help your people make this journey more deeply in their personal devotional life?

SPIRITUAL PRACTICES

Take a half-day (or longer) retreat at the beginning of each major season, and pray into the spiritual work of that season. For instance, Advent (pray your longings; pray how Christ is being formed in you); Lent (pray repentance and the work of dying to sin); Ordinary Time (pray calling; evaluate your Rule of Life).

Pray the weekly Collect from the Book of Common Prayer (pp. 211ff).

Use color and symbols to decorate your table, or your prayer place, according to the Church season. Let them remind you to pray the presence and work of Jesus that relates to that season.

A Prayer of Illumination:
Lord God, Heavenly Father, whose life is formed in us as we are formed in you, draw us so closely into the life and death and resurrected glory of Jesus that we find ourselves already living in Eternity now. This we pray in your Spirit, and through the Lord of all time, Jesus Christ. Amen.

54. ADVENT LONGING

SUSAN PORTERFIELD CURRIE

———◆———

Lo, in the silent night
A child to God is born
And all is brought again
That ere was lost or lorn.
Could but thy soul, O man,
Become a silent night!
God would be born in thee
And set all things aright.
(15th century, quoted in *Watch for the Light*)

At first glance, this is a Christmas poem. But what stirs inside us as we read it is not what's stirred by tinsel, colored lights, or packages under the tree. This poem invites us into mystery, into highly alert attentiveness as we watch to see eternity unfolding in reality. It evokes longing, in heart and soul and even body, and longing prays into hope.

To set all things aright… all that's lost, found; all that's lorn, welcomed into love. What an astounding and marvelous promise! It's the promise of God's ways in this world, held before us in the Scriptures and in time and place, history opening into eternity. It's the

Garden of Eden, restored; it's freedom from sin and all its effects, death overcome and darkness fleeing away. It's what God brings when he comes to live among us.

Advent—the season of the church year that begins 4 Sundays before Christmas—turns our eyes and ears, our hearts and prayers, toward the coming of the Lord: at Christmas, and again at the end of time. As wonderful as Christmas is, it celebrates only the Lord's first coming, and jumping into it too quickly denies us the opportunity to pray into his return, when all that Jesus began at his first coming will be completed. Like the faithful servants who wait and watch through the night for their master's return, keeping their lamps trimmed, we remain alert and attentive, praying with expectation the groaning of creation (Romans 8:18-27), giving it words in the last prayer in the Bible: Come, Lord Jesus! (Rev 22:20)

Praying our longings not only stewards the world but also shapes us for eternity. It is a spiritual discipline: the outward behavior (praying our longings) shapes the disposition of our hearts (arousing expectation), which shapes us in virtue (hope). And hope waits eagerly to be fulfilled, knowing that what longing has been shaping, eternity will invite us into enjoying.

It's like coming into the dining room after smelling the feast cooking for hours. We come in with our senses already aroused, and as we make our way along the table, we are able to pass by all that will not satisfy, knowing from our heightened senses how to identify what it is that the host has been lovingly preparing. And when our senses meet what it is that has been alerting them—ahh! A feast! Gloria!

As Advent begins, light your lamps. Turn toward the Lord's coming. And pray the longings of this groaning world, and of your deepest heart. Jesus is on his way to make all things right, as surely as the dawn breaks from on high.

"All around us we observe a pregnant creation. The difficult times of pain throughout the world are simply birth pangs. But it's not only around us; it's within us. The Spirit of God is arousing us within. We're also feeling the birth pangs. These sterile and barren bodies of ours are yearning for full deliverance. That is why waiting does not diminish us, any more than waiting diminishes a pregnant mother. We are enlarged in the waiting. We, of course, don't see what is enlarging us. But the longer we wait, the larger we become, and the more joyful our expectancy."
—Romans 8:22-25, The Message

"We not only wait for God; we wait with God."
—Gordon Giles, O Come Emmanuel

REJOICE! REJOICE, BELIEVERS
A HYMN BY LAURENTIUS LAURENTI, 1700, TRANS.
SARAH B. FINDLATER (1823-1907)

Rejoice! Rejoice, believers,
And let your lights appear;
The evening is advancing,
And darker night is near.
The Bridegroom is arising
And soon is drawing nigh.
Up, pray and watch and wrestle;
At midnight comes the cry.

See that your lamps are burning,
Replenish them with oil;
And wait for your salvation,
The end of sin and toil.
The marriage feast is waiting,
The gates wide open stand;
Arise, O heirs of glory,
The Bridegroom is at hand.

Our hope and expectation,
O Jesus, now appear;
Arise, O Sun so longed for,

O'er this benighted sphere.
With hearts and hands uplifted,
We plead, O Lord, to see
The day of earth's redemption
That sets your people free!

REFLECTION QUESTIONS

What's the difference between our wants and our longings or yearnings? How are we present in each? How is God present?

Romans 8 describes creation groaning, waiting to be set free (v. 22), our own groaning as we bodily await full redemption (v. 23), and the Holy Spirit groaning as he intercedes for us (v. 26). What does it look like for these groanings to interact with each other in prayer? How do verses 27 and 28 elaborate on the presence of God in these Advent prayers?

Given this understanding of Advent, how might you begin this holy season in ways that are about praying your holy longings and then watching in prayerful expectation?

SPIRITUAL PRACTICES

Watch, listen to, or read the news. Then hold all you're aware of before the Lord, noticing what longing is evoked. Pray three simple words: Come, Lord Jesus.

Journal your deepest longings. What would it look like for all to be right, and whole, and graced? Become present to the Lord's promised return and how that will make everything well and new, and pray again: Come, Lord Jesus.

Find a hymnal that's arranged by the church year, and pray the Advent hymns.

Each morning as you arise and become present to the day ahead and the world around, look toward the horizon and pray Psalm 130.

A Prayer of Illumination:
I wait for you, O Lord, my whole being waits, and in your Word I put my hope. I wait for you more than watchmen wait for the morning, more than watchmen wait for the morning. I put my hope in you, for with you is unfailing love, and with you is full redemption. Amen. (adapted from Psalm 130:5-7)

55. A CHILD-LIKE ADVENT

ANGELA WISDOM

———————◆———————

We sit on the floor keeping prayerful watch as the children around me do their work, responding to the Noah story in their private prayer and reflection time. They are quiet and focused. One is playing with figures and silently re-creating the story as she moves the figures about on her prayer rug. One boy is painting with watercolors, choosing dark blues and browns to depict the ark being tossed about in the waves. Later at home, a child says thoughtfully: "Mom, I wonder if they felt safe in the ark. There must have been poisonous snakes in there." "Hmm, now I wonder that too, son," his mother replies.

In the days prior, God had met us as we prepared to lead the children in worship via the Noah story. In the course of that fairly normal week, we had encountered the first- or second-hand impacts of despair, spiritual warfare, adultery, substance abuse, power abuse, pride, human trafficking, terminal illness and miscarriage. As we practiced and memorized the story, we considered the experience of Noah in the face of a crumbling world as he trusted God's Word and built the ark. We wondered about what it must have been like to be closed up inside as the storm approached. And by entering the story deeply, we shared in a part of the joy that Noah and his family and the animals must have felt as they exited the ark and stepped out into the wide open salvation space of a world made clean and new. This was a world that was to be their new home.

The capacity of children to pray and be open to God's revelation is astounding. Advent is the perfect season to reflect on the contribution children make to the formation of the wider Body of Christ. As our children grow, God is not just forming them in their own faith; he is also forming us in ours as we relate to one another. And their contribution is not limited to the factors we often cite, namely, that relating to children requires patience, sacrifice, and humility. No, Jesus said: "Truly I say to you, whoever does not receive the kingdom of God like a child shall not enter it" (Luke 18:17 ESV). Children have a great deal to teach us about spiritual formation and prayer, and God often makes the formation mutual when we are intentional about leading children in worship together. May this season of Advent be one where the children in our communities lead us to the manger with joy.

*"The wolf shall dwell with the lamb, and the leopard shall lie down with
the young goat, and the calf and the lion and the fattened calf together;
and a little child shall lead them."*
—Isaiah 11:6 ESV

*"Jesus called them back. 'Let these children alone. Don't get between them
and me. These children are the kingdom's pride and joy. Mark this:
Unless you accept God's kingdom in the simplicity of a child,
you'll never get in.'"*
—Luke 18:16-17, The Message

CHRISTIAN CHILDREN, ADVENT BIDS YOU
A HYMN BY ESTHER WIGLESWORTH, 1881

Christian children, Advent bids you
meet your Lord upon his way;
watch, for now the night is waning,
soon will dawn the endless day.

Christian children, Jesus bids you
daily pray "Thy kingdom come";
watch, and wait for his appearing
till he come to take you home.

Christian children, he anoints you
with his Spirit from above;
see then that your lamps be burning
with the fire of faith and love.

Christian children, when we think not
we shall hear the aweful cry,
"Go ye forth to meet the Bridegroom;
haste, for Jesus draweth nigh!"

Christian children, they shall meet him,
faithful children of the light;
they whose lamps are trimmed and burning,
and their garments pure and white.

O how blessed to fall before him!
O how blessed his praise to sing!
Love him, serve him, and adore him,
in the city of our King!

REFLECTION QUESTIONS

In what ways do you accept the kingdom of God with the simplicity of a child?

In what ways do you resist entering the kingdom of God with the simplicity of a child?

Do you pay attention to how God uses children as instruments of spiritual formation?

How are you investing in the spiritual nurture of children in your life?

How will you receive the gift of Advent with a child-like heart?

SPIRITUAL PRACTICES

Take this season as an opportunity to observe children in your proximity and enjoy how they relate to God, each other, and the wider Body of Christ.

Ask the Lord to give you a word of blessing and/or encouragement for a particular child and an opportunity to share it with that child for God's glory.

Volunteer your time to serve children through a social justice cause, a children's ministry, a friendship, or a discipleship relationship.

Journal some experiences you have had in which God used a child to impact your spiritual life.

A Prayer of Illumination:
Come, thou long-expected Jesus, born to set Thy people free; from our fears and sins release us, let us find our rest in Thee. Israel's strength and consolation, hope of all the earth Thou art; dear desire of every nation, joy of every longing heart. Born Thy people to deliver, born a child and yet a King, born to reign in us forever, now Thy gracious kingdom bring. By thine own eternal Spirit, rule in all our hearts alone, by thine all-;sufficient merit, raise us to Thy glorious throne. Amen. Charles Wesley

56. INCARNATION

RICK ANDERSON

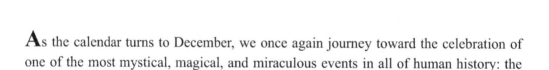

As the calendar turns to December, we once again journey toward the celebration of one of the most mystical, magical, and miraculous events in all of human history: the Incarnation. Emmanuel: "God with us." God came down. God with skin on. God in the flesh.

Many a sensationalized Hollywood film in recent years has attempted to capture the concept of gods in human skin: mighty, majestic, kingly - and always accessorized with lots of shiny accoutrements. But apparently none of those screenwriters paid attention in Sunday School. The real God who came to us in human form didn't arrive in that fashion at all. He came as a baby boy, a callused carpenter, a transfixing teacher, a humble healer, a wave-maker, a wave-calmer, and ultimately a suffering Savior. And in all of that, he came to live among us and make God known to us.

The presence of God in the Old Testament was too great for any man or woman to take. They collapsed, face to the ground, at the prospect of catching even a glimpse of God. But with the Incarnation, everything changed. The people of his creation could look God in the face, feel the touch of God's hand, be greeted with a holy kiss from the lips of God. That is the miracle of the Incarnation.

One wonders what it will be like when a person looks into the eyes of Jesus. Can you imagine it? What must it be like to look into the eyes of God and have him look back at you? We collectively assume something very special will happen. Jesus' gaze will have a gravity to it that makes one feel truly seen and deeply loved. We who know and love him look forward to finding out someday.

We also have to believe that Jesus is a great hugger. Hugs incarnate love and acceptance. But there's a broad spectrum of practitioners. Some people fully commit to a hug like they're making a plaster mold of themselves and they've only got one shot at it. Others hug as if they've just come in from the rain and are primarily concerned with not getting you wet. Great hugs are a simple but profound incarnational gift to share with humanity.

In his providence, God invites us to participate with him in a variety of ways - to be the arms and voice of God to one another and to the broken world around us. Each time we are a conduit of God's love, Emmanuel arrives again. Even now Jesus is coming to us - in the text from a friend saying they're thinking of us (reflecting the way God is mindful of us), in the hug when we're hurting or feeling alone (reflecting God's warmth and desire to hold us close), in the words of encouragement that lift our spirits (reflecting God's desire to see us emboldened and fully alive), and in the forgiveness offered by someone we've let down (reflecting God's goodness and grace).

When you accept Christ and receive the Holy Spirit, you become another instance of humanity that harbors God inside. Be alert to how you can be an incarnate vessel of God's love today. It's an ongoing miracle!

"The virgin will conceive and give birth to a son, and will call him Immanuel."
—Isaiah 7:14b

"The central miracle asserted by Christians is the Incarnation.
They say that God became Man. Every other miracle prepares for this,
or exhibits this, or results from this."
—C.S. Lewis

O COME, O COME, EMMANUEL
A HYMN BY JOHN MASON NEALE, 1851 (v. 1, 7, 8)

O come, O come, Emmanuel,
and ransom captive Israel
that mourns in lonely exile here
until the Son of God appear.
Rejoice! Rejoice! Emmanuel
shall come to you, O Israel.

O come, O Bright and Morning Star,
and bring us comfort from afar!
Dispel the shadows of the night
and turn our darkness into light.
Rejoice! Rejoice! Emmanuel
shall come to you, O Israel.

O come, O King of nations, bind
in one the hearts of all mankind.
Bid all our sad divisions cease
and be yourself our King of Peace.
Rejoice! Rejoice! Emmanuel
shall come to you, O Israel.

REFLECTION QUESTIONS

Read Matthew 8:1-4 and imagine yourself as the leper crying out to Jesus for healing. What happens in your soul when Jesus makes eye contact with you and says, "I am willing. Be clean!"?

What are small, practical ways in which you could go out of your way to incarnate God's love and kindness to a world that needs it so badly?

Have you taken for granted the incarnational vessel that you are? How can you be the arms and voice of God to those within your reach?

What could you do in this Advent season to focus your attention and anticipation on the coming of Emmanuel?

SPIRITUAL PRACTICES

Read the Beatitudes (Matthew 5:1-12) and picture yourself in the front row. Jesus is close enough to touch. Can you hear his voice? Can you make eye contact?

What gifts has God specifically given you to incarnate his love and presence: Words of encouragement? A peaceful and reassuring presence? The ability to spur others on? A compassionate heart? A healing touch? How can you use those gifts with more intentionality?

Hugs are a gift of incarnation. Practice. Practice. Practice.

Specifically endeavor to choose a stranger to "surprise with kindness" in the next 48 hours. How will you do it?

A Prayer of Illumination:
Lord Jesus, thank you for descending into lowly humanity to show us what God is like and how he feels about us. Help us to receive that gift afresh this December. Attune our senses to all the opportunities we have each day to incarnate your love and grace and kindness to those we love and those we've never met. With gratitude for the gift of Emmanuel, Amen.

57. CHRISTMAS PRESENCE

STEPHEN A. MACCHIA

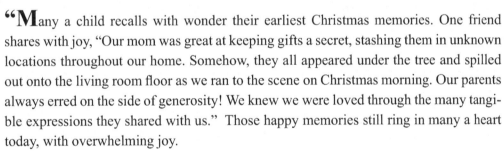

"**M**any a child recalls with wonder their earliest Christmas memories. One friend shares with joy, "Our mom was great at keeping gifts a secret, stashing them in unknown locations throughout our home. Somehow, they all appeared under the tree and spilled out onto the living room floor as we ran to the scene on Christmas morning. Our parents always erred on the side of generosity! We knew we were loved through the many tangible expressions they shared with us." Those happy memories still ring in many a heart today, with overwhelming joy.

What will you give…and get…for Christmas? This is the FAQ of the month! We tend to equate Christmas with gift-giving and receiving, and for good reason. God himself set the example for us. He generously sent to earth his one and only Son, Jesus, the greatest gift of all and for all. We commemorate this most amazing gift by offering each other tangible expressions of our love each Christmas. 'Tis the season!

For the next four weeks, we can prepare best for all the Christmas *presents* when we also prepare our hearts for his loving *presence.* Known as Advent, it ironically commences on the heels of Black Friday, one of the busiest shopping *daze* (!) of the year. However, Advent is to be a season of hopeful anticipation, of waiting and watching once more to witness the wonder of the Incarnation: Jesus' first advent in the lowly manger of Bethlehem. We remember with childlike faith this humble beginning, in each Advent season of our earthly lives, in anticipation of his coming again in all his glory at the Second Advent, when Christ ushers us in eternity.

In addition to the presents you plan to share with another, will you notice as well the gift of God's presence – in worship, in community, and in your prayer closet? How about the attentive presence you can offer to another as a spiritual friend? And what about the listening presence you can offer to your own heart and soul in quietness and rest? This kind of *presence* is far more precious than any tangible *present* we give to or receive from another.

Receiving from God the gifts of his hope-filled presence will undoubtedly shape the way you discern, purchase. and give presents to others. The gifts of presence that God desires to offer freely and generously to you are to be received fully with an open heart and outstretched arms.

When God's presence and your presence are offered to others in that same prayerfully charitable posture, gift-giving comes alive in the Spirit, brings joy to the Father, renews focus on our Savior Jesus, and builds up God's Kingdom here on earth and for all eternity.

Don't miss out on God's loving presence for your own soul. Be sure to behold the coming of the Lord in the love of the Christ Child, and then become for others what you've more fully received for yourself. As you wait with expectancy, watch with hopefulness, wonder with joyfulness, and witness with delight, may this Advent and Christmas become one of your best ever.

"The Word became flesh and made his dwelling among us.
We have seen his glory, the glory of the one and only Son,
who came from the Father, full of grace and truth."
—John 1:14

COME, THOU LONG EXPECTED JESUS
A HYMN BY CHARLES WESLEY, 1745

Come, thou long expected Jesus,
born to set thy people free;
from our fears and sins release us,
let us find our rest in thee.

Israel's strength and consolation,
hope of all the earth thou art;
dear desire of every nation,
joy of every longing heart.

Born thy people to deliver,
born a child and yet a King,
born to reign in us forever,
now thy gracious kingdom bring.

By thine own eternal Spirit
rule in all our hearts alone;
by thine all sufficient merit,
raise us to thy glorious throne.

REFLECTION QUESTIONS

Waiting: Read Psalm 16…what does the psalmist suggest about waiting in our journey?

Watching: Read Isaiah 9:1-7…what are the people of God watching for in the future?

Wondering: Read Luke 1:46-55…what is Mary wondering about in her soul?

Witnessing: Read Luke 1:67-79…what is Zechariah giving witness to in his song?

SPIRITUAL PRACTICES

Waiting: In the 1st week of Advent, find at least one 10-15 minute block of time to sit silently in solitude. Ponder the word *wait* and consider how well/poorly you "wait" in life.

Watching: In the 2nd week of Advent, notice at least 3-5 gifts of God's presence embracing you in love, awakening you with wisdom, or offering you his companionship through another.

Wondering: In the 3rd week of Advent, pause for one full hour. Journal or sketch as many of God's good gifts as you can, as part of preparing your heart for Christmas.

Witnessing: In the 4th week of Advent, consider adding a special note to your gifts, sharing with loved ones a simple prayer that God's loving presence will be especially near.

A Prayer of Illumination:
Heavenly Father, thank you for sending your Son, Jesus, miraculously into this world, and for gifting us with the presence of your Holy Spirit to guide, protect, sustain, and transform us in this Advent and Christmas season. Amen.

58. EPIPHANY

SUSAN PORTERFIELD CURRIE

---◆---

Let's do a word association. "Epiphany" – what do you think?

Likely it's "the wise men!" And indeed, Epiphany day—January 6th, the day after the 12th day of Christmas—commemorates the arrival of the wise men bearing gifts for the infant Jesus.

As such, it celebrates God's self-revelation--not only to his people Israel (Jesus' family, the shepherds, Simeon and Anna, and any others listening in on the stories told in and around Bethlehem and Jerusalem those first several weeks and months), but now out to the Gentile peoples of the world as well. Likely the magi were the first missionary evangelists, returning to their own Eastern countries with the news of the Incarnation!

The word *epiphany* itself means "revelation," a manifestation of reality, as in "I've had an epiphany!" And thus January 6th, while celebrating the arrival and generosity of the magi from afar, is just the beginning of the entire season of the church year sometimes called Epiphanytide—the weeks lasting up to the beginning of Lent. During the Sundays of Epiphanytide, the Scripture readings focus on the stories of Jesus' revelation—his baptism in the river Jordan by John, God the Father himself revealing the identity of Jesus: "This is my Son, whom I love!" (Matthew 3:17); continuing with the wedding at Cana—"the first of the signs through which he revealed his glory," John tells us (John 2:11); and going on to look at accounts of Jesus' early ministry in Galilee, revealing himself in word and deed to be the Messiah. In the middle of the season we read of the presentation of the forty-day-old Jesus in the Temple, when by the Spirit faithful Anna is able to see in Jesus the redemption of Jerusalem, and devout Simeon proclaims, "My eyes have seen your salvation, which you have prepared in the sight of all nations: a light for revelation to the Gentiles, and the glory of your people Israel!" (Luke 2:22-38)

The season of Epiphany culminates in the Feast of the Transfiguration. Jesus, turning his face toward the cross (and thus we with him, preparing to journey there through Lent), takes his inner circle of Peter, John, and James up onto a mountain to pray. While praying, he is transfigured before them and his full glory is revealed visibly—"his face shone like the sun" (Matthew 17), his clothes "became as bright as a flash of lightning" (Luke 9), becoming "dazzling white" (Mark 9)—while the voice of God the Father reveals Jesus' identity in spoken word: "This is my Beloved Son; listen to him!"

Thus what's being revealed at Epiphany—to the faithful, and to the nations—is Jesus, God incarnate amongst us, shining his glory upon us. As we bring our gifts—our offering of ourselves, body and soul, gazing upon him in worship, we, too, are being transformed into his glorious image (2 Cor 3:18). "Glory!" we breathe, and fall on our knees before Christ, the Light of the world.

"Arise, shine, for your light has come,
and the glory of the Lord rises upon you.
See, darkness covers the earth
and thick darkness is over the peoples,
but the Lord rises upon you
and his glory appears over you.
Nations will come to your light,
and kings to the brightness of your dawn . . .
the Lord will be your everlasting light,
and your God will be your glory."
—Isaiah 60:1-3, 19

"As those who see light are in the light sharing its brilliance,
so those who see God are in God sharing his glory, and that glory gives them life.
To see God is to share in life."
—Irenaeus, A Treatise Against Heresies, 130-200 A.D.

SONGS OF THANKFULNESS AND PRAISE
A HYMN BY CHRISTOPHER WORDSWORTH, 1862

Songs of thankfulness and praise, Jesus, Lord, to thee we raise,
Manifested by the star to the sages from afar;
Branch of royal David's stem, in thy birth at Bethlehem:
Anthems be to thee addressed, God in man made manifest.

Manifest at Jordan's stream, Prophet, Priest, and King supreme;
And at Cana, wedding guest, in thy Godhead manifest;
Manifest in power divine, changing water into wine:
Anthems be to thee addressed, God in man made manifest.

Manifest in making whole palsied limbs and fainting soul;
Manifest in valiant fight, quelling all the devil's might;
Manifest in gracious will, ever bringing good from ill:
Anthems be to thee addressed, God in man made manifest.

Sun and moon shall darkened be, stars shall fall, the heavens shall flee;
Christ will then like lightning shine, all will see his glorious sign;
All will then the trumpet hear, all will see the Judge appear:
Thou by all wilt be confessed, God in man made manifest.

Grant us grace to see thee, Lord, mirrored in thy holy Word;
May we imitate thee now, and be pure, as pure art thou;
That we like to thee may be at thy great Epiphany;
And may praise thee, ever blest, God in man made manifest.

REFLECTION QUESTIONS

How did God reveal his presence to you this day? Notice, and give thanks.

When today were you given glimpses of God's glory? Notice, and breathe "glory!"

In the verses below, characterizing the truths of Epiphany (the Lord's self-revelation, light, glory) how do you experience these truths in your own life with God?

1 Peter 1:20

John 1:9, 14

John 2:11

1 John 1:1-7

Revelation 21:22-26

SPIRITUAL PRACTICES

Keep your fireside stockings up through the twelve days of Christmas, filling them with loose change each day. On Epiphany, collect the change and give it to a mission cause (bringing Christ to the nations, a tradition begun at the first Epiphany).

Light a candle at twilight to remind you of Christ's light shining in the darkness, revealing his presence to the world. As you do so, pray or sing the *Phos Hilaron,* one of the earliest hymns of the church:

> *O gladsome light,*
> *pure brightness of the everliving Father in heaven,*
> *O Jesus Christ, holy and blessed!*
> *Now as we come to the setting of the sun,*
> *and our eyes behold the vesper light,*
> *we sing your praises, O God: Father, Son, and Holy Spirit.*
> *You are worthy at all times to be praised by happy voices,*
> *O Son of God, O Giver of Life,*
> *and to be glorified through all the worlds.*

A Prayer of Illumination:

Almighty God, whose Son our Savior Jesus Christ is the light of the world: Grant that your people may shine with the radiance of Christ's glory, that he may be known, worshiped, and obeyed to the ends of the earth; through Jesus Christ our Lord, who reigns with you and the Holy Spirit, one God, now and forever. Amen.

Book of Common Prayer, Anglican Church in North America, 2019, p. 602

59. LENT: A SEASON OF PREPARATION

STEPHEN A. MACCHIA

---◇---

Although not observed by all Protestants, Lent is considered an important season of preparation for Easter by Methodist, Presbyterian, Lutheran, and Anglican denominations. In addition, Catholic and Orthodox churches signify Lent as a 40-day journey (not including Sundays) from Ash Wednesday to Easter. It's a time set aside for the church to anticipate prayerfully and reverently the signature event of our faith in Jesus Christ: his death on the cross and his miraculous resurrection from the dead.

For many others, Holy Week is the sole emphasis of Lent... from the triumphal entry of Jesus into Jerusalem on the back of a donkey on Palm Sunday, through the events of Christ's final week on earth, including such notables as Peter's denial, Judas's betrayal, foot washing, the Last Supper, the Garden of Gethsemane, Jesus' arrest, the crucifixion, and the empty tomb of Easter Resurrection. The culmination of Jesus' earthly ministry is the epicenter of our Christian faith, and his Resurrection is what gives us hope for all eternity.

Jesus' outstretched arms of love on the cross are such a wonderful symbol of why he came to earth. As a member of the Trinity, the Son of God was sent as a once-and-for-all sacrifice for our sins. His love was evidenced in our midst and on our behalf, so that no longer would there need to be the offering of a bull or lamb to settle that matter for us before Almighty God. Because of the Lord's deep love for his children worldwide,

Jesus came to bear witness to the miraculous and eternal message of love, show forth evidences of his redemptive love, and invite others to follow him from the lowly manger to the humble cross and with him into heaven. What a gift of hope and joy, peace and love…from God to us! Alleluia!

Will you participate in Lent yourself or among your faith community? Are you planning to "give up" something for this season, to signify your own personal journey of self-sacrifice and accompaniment with Jesus to the cross? Or, are you going to "add" something to your Christian life, perhaps including a new spiritual discipline, such as fasting, or following a set of readings offered via the web or in a devotional book?

Whatever your stance may be toward the season of Lent, we trust that the days preceding and including Easter will be filled to overflowing with penitential humility and reverential joy. Christ the Lord was sent to our planet to walk and serve among us, and to suffer and die on our behalf, so that we too can share the delight of worship and fellowship with God for all eternity. Whether that prompts you to fall on your knees and prayerfully surrender some aspect of your life, or whether it brings you to your feet with worshipful desire to love and please him in new ways, our prayer is that Lent will be rich in meaning for you and yours.

*"The season of Lent may be the most emotionally charged
season of the Christian year."*
—Rueben Job

*"What we are called to give up in Lent is control
itself...and lay down (surrender) my resistance to the
One who loves me infinitely more than I can guess,
the One who is more on my side than I am myself."*
—Martin L. Smith, SSJE

I CANNOT TELL
A HYMN BY WILLIAM Y. FULLERTON, 1885-1932

I cannot tell why He whom angels worship
Should set His love upon the sons of men,
Or why, as Shepherd, He should seek the wanderers,
To bring them back, they know not how or when.
But this I know, that He was born of Mary
When Bethlehem's manger was His only home,
And that He lived at Nazareth and labored,
And so the Savior, Savior of the world is come.

I cannot tell how silently He suffered,
As with His peace He graced this place of tears,
Or how His heart upon the cross was broken,
The crown of pain to three and thirty years.
But this I know, He heals the brokenhearted,
And stays our sin, and calms our lurking fear,
And lifts the burden from the heavy laden,
For yet the Savior, Savior of the world is here.

I cannot tell how He will win the nations,
How He will claim His earthly heritage,
How satisfy the needs and aspirations
Of East and West, of sinner and of sage.
But this I know, all flesh shall see His glory,
And He shall reap the harvest He has sown,
And some glad day His sun shall shine in splendor
When He the Savior, Savior of the world is known.

I cannot tell how all the lands shall worship,
When, at His bidding, every storm is stilled,
Or who can say how great the jubilation
When all the hearts of men with love are filled.
But this I know, the skies will thrill with rapture,
And myriad, myriad human voices sing,
And earth to Heaven, and Heaven to earth, will answer:
At last the Savior, Savior of the world is King!

REFLECTION QUESTIONS

What is your personal view of Lent? Is it a time to focus your heart, mind, and soul on preparing for Holy Week and Easter? If so, how?

Why is it meaningful to give up (an appetite, attitude, or action) or add to (spiritual practice such as fasting or Lenten devotional) your Lenten experience?

In what ways will you live more humbly and sacrificially during this Lenten season, not just for personal piety but to reflect Jesus' outstretched arms of love to your world?

How do you respond to the following words: surrender; sacrifice; suffering; humility; brokenness? In what ways do these words belong in our Lenten vocabulary?

SPIRITUAL PRACTICES

Spend additional time in your prayer closet during Lent. Invite the Spirit of God to move your heart deeply by reflecting on the Gospel passages which focus on Jesus' final days on earth.

Consider unplugging from technology or giving up something you particularly enjoy, in order to "feel" the struggle of letting go and connecting with the meaning of sacrifice.

Travel with Jesus during Holy Week, focusing your biblical reflections on the following events: Palm Sunday; Clearing the Temple; Greatest Commandment; Parable of the Ten Talents; Foot Washing and Lord's Supper; Peter's Denial; Judas's Betrayal; Garden of Gethsemane; Arrest; Crucifixion; Burial; Resurrection.

A Prayer of Illumination:
God, forbid that I should boast except in the cross of our Lord Jesus Christ, for it is no longer I who live, but the Risen Christ lives in me; and the life which I now live in the flesh I live by faith in the Son of God, who loved me and gave Himself for me. Amen.
(Galatians 6:14; 2:20)

60. LENT - A TRAIL OF TEARS

ANGELA WISDOM

———◇———

Lent is a weighty time of year when we are invited to enter into our brokenness and our need for Christ. It is a time to pray for healing for ourselves, our families, our communities, and our world. It is a time when we become acutely aware of our grief, our regrets, our limitations, our lament. It is also a time when we learn most deeply that we are not alone.

In the mystery of the Kingdom, we find that we walk with Jesus and he walks with us in our suffering and brokenness. When we learn that we are not alone, we need not fear attending to our sorrow, because we know that there is a High Priest who helps us in our weakness. We can "then with confidence draw near to the throne of grace, that we may receive mercy and find grace to help in time of need." (Hebrews 4:16)

Recently our family spent a few days in Shawnee National Forest. Little did we know that such a lush area of beautiful rock outcroppings, waterfalls, and wildlife abuts the Southern border of our level agricultural Midwestern landscape. In the middle of this beautiful forest topography lies a significant portion of what remains of the Trail of Tears, the route traveled by Cherokee, Seminole, Chickasaw, and Chocktaw among other tribes of Native Americans, as they were forcefully relocated from their lush homeland to the West from 1830-1850. The "tears" weren't just the grief of injustice and the loss of their land. The "tears" were the disease, exposure, and loss of life experienced by these souls as they made this trek. Thousands died along the way. It sobers me, and rightly so. As we contemplate the sorrow of this trail winding through the preserved forest beauty, we remember that in this life of sorrows and of joys, we have hope because Jesus walks this "trail of tears" with us. We are not alone.

What is the purpose of giving attention to things we are powerless to change? It's an important question. We put away our "Alleluias" and identification with the unlimited resources available in the Kingdom and allow ourselves to remember our limitations and failures. There are circumstances out of our control, fractured relationships we cannot mend, and regrets that nag our souls, and dull our sensitivities. To ignore these will lead to a superficial faith, stunt our maturity, and cheapen grace. During Lent, we return to God with fasting, tears, and lament. We "rend our hearts . . . for he is gracious and merciful, slow to anger, and abounding in steadfast love" (Joel 2:12-13). We engage in confession, release our idols, and let go of disordered attachments, that we may be restored to life-giving relationships with God and with others. Let us embrace the mystery of Christ with us as we journey toward Passion Week.

"Return to the LORD your God, for he is gracious and merciful,
slow to anger, and abounding in steadfast love."
—Joel 2:13

"What does love look like? It has the hands to help others. It has the feet to hasten to
the poor and needy. It has eyes to see misery and want. It has the ears to hear the sighs
and sorrows of men. That is what love looks like."
—Augustine of Hippo

COME YE SINNERS, POOR AND NEEDY
A HYMN BY JOSEPH HART, 1759 (vv. 1-3)

Come, ye sinners, poor and needy,
Weak and wounded, sick and sore;
Jesus ready stands to save you,
Full of pity, love and pow'r.

Refrain:
I will arise and go to Jesus,
He will embrace me in His arms;
In the arms of my dear Savior,
Oh, there are ten thousand charms.

Come, ye thirsty, come, and welcome,
God's free bounty glorify;
True belief and true repentance,
Every grace that brings you nigh.

Come, ye weary, heavy-laden,
Lost and ruined by the fall;
If you tarry till you're better,
You will never come at all.

REFLECTION QUESTIONS

Is there anything in your life that you are grieving or need to grieve? How might you make room this Lent to honor your grief, aware of Christ's presence with you in your sense of loss?

Do you or your loved ones need physical, emotional, or relational healing? How might God be bringing about healing in some areas of your life as the result of brokenness in other areas of your life? For instance, perhaps a physical illness has brought about deeper relational intimacy with those most dear to you. Or perhaps an area of sin has brought about humility and repentance.

Are there circumstances or relationships that cause heartache and put you in touch with your limitations and your need for Christ? Allow yourself to attend to your sorrow and remember Jesus as you entrust these matters to God in faith.

For whom in your community has God given you eyes of love to see their sighs and sorrows? Is there an invitation to be a source of God's comfort and hope during these forty days of Lent?

SPIRITUAL PRACTICES

In your personal journey:

Simplify your meals and activities to make room for what is most important.

Release any disordered attachments to habits, people, or things in order that you might rightly relate to God, others, and the created world.

Meditate on Matthew 13:31-32. How will you make room for the "mustard seed" of the Kingdom of God to grow in your life and context?

In your faith community:

Organize an intentional time of prayer for healing with your family, friends, small group, church, or community. Practice confession and reconciliation.

As you observe communion this Lenten season, open yourself more deeply to the love and companionship of Christ in your sighs and sorrows.

Are there any global concerns that capture your attention? How might your concerns stir you to action on behalf of a person or group suffering from hopelessness, poverty, or injustice?

A Prayer of Illumination:

Oh God, you who are gracious and merciful, slow to anger and abounding in steadfast love, deepen our trust and devotion to you and to your Kingdom this Lenten season. Give us your eyes of love to see not only our own sorrow, but the sighs and sorrows of others in our communities, and in the world around us. May this season be one of healing and hope as we return to you--our source of life, salvation, and joy. In Christ's Name and for his glory. Amen.

61. EASTER RESURRECTION

JEREMY STEFANO

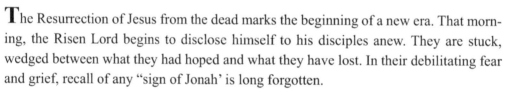

The Resurrection of Jesus from the dead marks the beginning of a new era. That morning, the Risen Lord begins to disclose himself to his disciples anew. They are stuck, wedged between what they had hoped and what they have lost. In their debilitating fear and grief, recall of any "sign of Jonah' is long forgotten.

On that day and the days that follow, Jesus appears among them and speaks to his beleaguered band of disciples. He names the dilemmas that have disoriented them, and he masterfully questions them, calling out the dated perspective of their troubles. "Woman, why are you weeping?" he asks gently. His compassionate enquiry, "Why are you troubled?" brings up new questions, as do the words, "Why do doubts arise in your heart?" since he is the One standing before them. In the same way, he brings Peter back to where they had left off: "Simon, son of John, do you love me?" Each time, his questions strike the nerve of their uncertainty, their confusion, while giving them space to consider the options.

Whatever their bewildered response may have been to the recent events, each person is offered opportunity to re-engage in Jesus' mission. In this way he calls forth, as from a tomb, their flagging faith. "Go and tell my brethren," he says to Mary. The dispirited disciples on the road to Emmaus are asked about their burden. "O foolish men, slow of heart to believe," he remarks, then causes their hearts to burn with the truth so strong that they run without being sent. "Peace be with you," he says to them all, and "Receive the Holy Spirit." To us who look in on those days from afar, his words ring still: "Do not be unbelieving but believing."

The post-Resurrection teachings of Jesus are concise and are of unparalleled authority, as only the Son of God, victorious over death, could be empowered to speak. He conscripts the disciples into his service, announcing, "Those whose sins you forgive, are forgiven," and "All authority in heaven and earth has been given to Me. Go. Make disciples of all nations, baptizing them in the name of the Father and of the Son and of the Holy Spirit, teaching them to keep all that I have commanded you. I am with you through all the days, to the very end of the age."

Then one day he is permanently taken from their sight, and the disciples are left to assimilate the new revelation about Jesus into their thinking and their living. With convincing proofs, he has demonstrated to them that he is risen from the dead, in a body like the one he had, yet not like it at all. He is risen indeed and remains with them, though unseen. And they are under his authority, commissioned to speak forgiveness, to baptize the believing, and to make disciples of people everywhere in his name.

"After his suffering, he presented himself to them and gave many convincing proofs that he was alive. He appeared to them over a period of forty days and spoke about the kingdom of God."
—Acts 1:3

"For me the most radical demand of Christian faith lies in summoning the courage to say yes to the present risenness of Jesus Christ."
—Brennan Manning, Abba's Child

CHRIST THE LORD IS RISEN TODAY
A HYMN BY CHARLES WESLEY, 1739

Christ the Lord is risen today, Alleluia!
Earth and heaven in chorus say, Alleluia!
Raise your joys and triumphs high, Alleluia!
Sing, ye heavens, and earth reply, Alleluia!

Love's redeeming work is done, Alleluia!
Fought the fight, the battle won, Alleluia!
Death in vain forbids him rise, Alleluia!
Christ has opened paradise, Alleluia!

Lives again our glorious King, Alleluia!
Where, O death, is now thy sting? Alleluia!
Once he died our souls to save, Alleluia!
Where's thy victory, boasting grave? Alleluia!

Soar we now where Christ has led, Alleluia!
Following our exalted Head, Alleluia!
Made like him, like him we rise, Alleluia!
Ours the cross, the grave, the skies, Alleluia!

REFLECTION QUESTIONS:

Does the reality of Jesus' Resurrection shape your perspective when praying alone or when you are active in ministry?

Is it all right if you're sometimes doubtful, sometimes believing, like the disciples?

In what way does Jesus' Resurrection impact how you think about your own body?

What is your part in the Great Commission?

SPIRITUAL PRACTICES:

Nurture awareness in your life that Christ is indeed risen and present with you in the "here and now." Notice his presence today.

Worship and pray with faith in the knowledge that Jesus lives and intercedes for you.

Listen for the prompting of the Spirit of Jesus to "go and tell" others that he lives.

Make a time and place to attend to Jesus' way of re-orienting your heart amidst your varied experiences of loss.

A Prayer of Illumination:
O God, who on this day, through your Only Begotten Son, have conquered death and unlocked for us the path to eternity, grant that we, through the renewal brought by your Spirit, may rise up in the light of life. Through our Lord Jesus Christ, your Son. Amen. (Easter Collect)

62. ASCENSION

JEREMY STEFANO

$\mathbf{F}$orty days after the resurrection, Jesus led his eleven disciples to a hilltop in the vicinity of Bethany on the Mount of Olives. There he spoke to them and lifted up his hands to bless them. As he was doing so, his body was lifted up and was carried upward until a cloud hid him from their sight. Enraptured, the disciples stood, their eyes fixed on the holy cloud in awe and worship. Two angels had to explain what had just happened. Jesus had been taken into heaven. They were to return to Jerusalem to await the coming of Holy Spirit.

This moment in history was not a mere enactment, symbolic or otherwise, revealing where heaven is. It was the literal fulfillment of Jesus' words: "I am going to him who sent me" (John 16:5). It was the day Jesus departed, in his human/spiritual body, from this dimension of human experience. He is not to be seen again until he comes on the clouds of heaven with glory. It would be some time before the apostles could incorporate into their understanding what had just happened to Jesus.

From the New Testament, a depiction of what this meant for Jesus can be pieced together. There was his return to the sanctuary not made with human hands, his glorification and restoration of authority at the Father's behest. And there were the subjection of all things under his feet, the sending of the Holy Spirit upon the praying disciples, the commencement of building his church, his ongoing intercession for the saints, and his preparation of a place for those who love and believe in him.

Being a Christian encompasses more than believing these things took place; it involves sharing in, or participating in, what God has brought about in Christ. Those who call on the name of Jesus are given life in him, being raised from death by participation with Jesus through baptism in his Resurrection. Being *in Christ* allows the believer to be with Jesus wherever he goes. Since Jesus ascended to heaven, the believer also is there with him, which is why Paul writes, "And God raised us up with Christ and seated us with him in the heavenly realms in Christ Jesus" (Ephesians 2:6). So even while we remain here on earth, we enjoy direct access to the Father in the Spirit.

What are we to make of such things, blessed as we are with every spiritual blessing *in the heavenlies*? We too might stand gazing up to heaven in awe and worship. To aid believers in realizing what God has done for us in Christ, Paul teaches, "… set your hearts on things above, where Christ is, seated at the right hand of God. Set your minds on things above, not on earthly things. For you died, and your life is now hidden with Christ in God. When Christ, who is your life, appears, then you also will appear with him in glory." (Colossians 3:1b-4)

"For Christ did not enter a sanctuary made with human hands
that was only a copy of the true one; he entered heaven itself,
now to appear for us in God's presence."
—Hebrews 9:24

"For Calvin, ascent was more than a metaphor: it was the decisive and
final action of Jesus Christ into which we are included and, as such,
is the foundation of his doctrine of participation. Ascent not only represents
the moment when the human Jesus was taken up to his Father
but also when all humanity is opened to this relationship as well."
—Julie Canlis, Calvin's Ladder: A Spiritual Theology of Ascent and Ascension

A HYMN OF GLORY LET US SING!
A HYMN BY THE VENERABLE BEDE, EIGHTH CENTURY

A hymn of glory let us sing!
Now hymns throughout the world shall ring.
Christ, by a road before untrod,
ascends unto the throne of God.
Alleluia! Alleluia!

The holy apostolic band
upon the Mount of Olives stand,
and with his faithful followers see
their Lord ascend in majesty.
Alleluia! Alleluia!

O Lord, our homeward pathway bend
that our unwearied hearts ascend,
where, seated on your Father's throne,
you reign as King of kings alone.
Alleluia! Alleluia!

O risen Christ, ascended Lord,
all praise to you let earth accord:
You are, while endless ages run,
with Father and with Spirit one.
Alleluia! Alleluia!

REFLECTION QUESTIONS:

Where is heaven?

How can one keep one's mind and heart set on heavenly things?

Why is it significant that Jesus' body was not left in the tomb and then later ascended into heaven?

Does the ascension of Jesus influence how a Christian intercedes in prayer?

SPIRITUAL PRACTICES:

Find ways to use the members of your earthly body that express and bear witness to who you are in Christ.

Pray the Lord's Prayer with the ascension in view, and notice where you are now seated in Christ.

Be in awe of what God has done today, and give thanks to the Lord for his abundant blessings.

Think about heaven. Perhaps making a list of specific people you are looking forward to meeting there may make this consideration less abstract.

A Prayer of Illumination:

Lift up your heads, you gates; be lifted up, you ancient doors,
that the King of glory may come in.
Who is this King of glory? The LORD strong and mighty,
the LORD mighty in battle.
Lift up your heads, you gates; lift them up, you ancient doors,
that the King of glory may come in.
Who is he, this King of glory?
The LORD Almighty – he is the King of glory.
Psalm 24:7-10

63. PENTECOST: WAITING ATTENTIVELY

SUZ SKINNER

Pentecost, or the Feast of Weeks, was an Old Testament appointed festival celebrating God's provision in the harvest, which included a "first fruits" offering to be made seven weeks (50 days) after the Passover Sabbath. Pentecost is also the name Christians use for an important New Testament historical event that took place after Jesus' death and resurrection, 50 days after the Passover. It was the day in which the promised Holy Spirit (Joel 2: 28-32) was poured out upon Jesus' disciples who were waiting in Jerusalem, during the Pentecost festival. Read the whole story from Acts 1: 4-14; 2:1-41.

Two elements are found in both OT and NT Pentecost which might help to reshape us and enable us to be more receptive to God's transforming work in our lives and in the world.

One element of Pentecost is that of *waiting attentively.* Waiting, in regards to our spiritual formation, may seem inactive or unproductive on the outside, but can be quite active within our souls. Waiting periods, when they are prayerful and attentive, are full of opportunities for learning trust, practicing humility, and releasing our need to control.

The OT harvest theme of Pentecost reminds us that the long dormant seed-in-the-ground waiting of winter and the slow and steady patience of spring flourishing always precede the abundance of harvest. Similarly, our spiritual formation requires attentive periods of rest and waiting, as well as patience with the slow process of growth and stretching, before we experience its fruit.

The NT command of Jesus to his disciples to wait in the city "until you have been clothed with power from on high" (Luke 24:49) reminds us to pay attention. Many times, seasons of waiting invite us to see the ways we are trying to do things in our own power and in our own way, rather than trusting in the power of God's Spirit. Whether the Holy Spirit comes with the sound of a mighty wind or in our quiet contemplation, Pentecost invites us to wait on the Lord, release control, and learn the freedom of trusting in God.

Another element of Pentecost is that of *being given*. This element involves action--action that is birthed out of waiting on the Lord. As we ponder the description of OT Pentecost harvest celebration (Leviticus 23: 9-22), we notice the "first fruits" were *being given* as a thank offering to God. Like the harvested grain given to the Lord, we can choose to live a life of *being given*, as a thank offering for God's gifts of Jesus and the Holy Spirit. On the day of Pentecost, Peter was *given* as he boldly stood up to address the crowds, speaking the truth, and bearing witness simply to what he knew and what he had seen. The other disciples, who were filled with the Holy Spirit, were *given* as they declared the wonders of God in other languages to the foreigners in the city. As God stirs our hearts and the Spirit fills us with gratitude, we will also respond to God's invitation to participate in the harvest work that the Spirit is doing in the world to bring people to himself. Pentecost can teach us to risk stepping out of our comfortable places, reach across cultural barriers in our own neighborhoods or afar, and choose to live a life of *being given* for the Kingdom of God.

"I wait for the Lord, my whole being waits,
and in his word I put my hope.
I wait for the Lord
more than watchmen wait for the morning,
more than watchmen wait for the morning.
Israel, put your hope in the Lord,
for with the Lord is unfailing love
and with him is full redemption.
He himself will redeem Israel
from all their sins."
—Psalm 130: 5-8

"Therefore, I urge you, brothers and sisters, in view of God's mercy,
to offer your bodies as a living sacrifice, holy and pleasing to God—this is your true
and proper worship."
—Romans 12:1

Communities of faith find life not by racing headlong into action, though action
almost always comes. They find their life by waiting...waiting on the power of a Holy
Spirit who is utterly beyond themselves and utterly real.
—Stephen V. Doughty, Weavings: Volume XIV, May/June 1999

GRACIOUS SPIRIT, DWELL WITH ME
A HYMN BY THOMAS T. LYNCH, 1855

Gracious Spirit, dwell with me;
I myself would gracious be;
And with words that help and heal
Would thy life in mine reveal;
And with actions bold and meek
Would for Christ my Savior speak.

Truthful Spirit, dwell with me;
I myself would truthful be;
And with wisdom kind and clear
Let thy life in mine appear;
And with actions brotherly
Speak my Lord's sincerity.

REFLECTION QUESTIONS

Have you noticed a particular situation, relationship, or desire that has been a place of waiting for you? What would it look like for you to be more attentive to God in your waiting?

In your desire to be filled with the power of the Spirit, are you willing to be stretched and humbled by the Holy Spirit?

In what ways has Jesus modeled for you a life of *being given*? In what ways is God inviting you to *be given* with the people he has put in your life?

What opportunities has God afforded you to be his witness, to reach across lines of differences with God's love and the good news of Jesus?

What gets in the way of following through with what God is putting on your heart? What gives you strength and courage?

SPIRITUAL PRACTICES

Read over Acts 1 and 2 prayerfully and with holy imagination. Place yourself in the scene from various viewpoints. Does this narrative move you in any way? Take what you are noticing into a quiet space with God, talking to him and listening to his heart

Soak in Psalm 130 together with a spiritual friend. Slowly read it several times aloud with one another, praying the words and letting them shape and form a personal prayer about waiting for the Lord. Write your own psalm to the Lord about waiting and trusting in him, and share it with your friend as you pray together.

Various postures in prayer can open the heart of the one praying in new ways. As God puts a seeker or unbeliever on your heart, pray for that person in a *given*, cruciform position. As you posture your desire to *be given*, with open arms, does praying this way shed light on anything God wants to show you about *being given* and trusting him?

A Prayer of Illumination:

Oh Lord, teach us how to wait upon you. In our places of waiting, shape us with humility and trust. With the presence of your Holy Spirit within, empower us to be your witnesses in this world as you work to bring in your harvest. Enable us to live a life of being given and may it be a thank offering that is pleasing to you. Amen.

64. ORDINARY TIME

DIANA CURREN BENNETT

We often look forward to celebrations, festivities, and joyous times together. Yet when all is over—decorations down, food consumed, and life resumed as we know it-- excitement wanes and perhaps a sense of the mundane resurfaces.

Similar situations arise with the church calendar. Our church year starts with Advent, the anticipation of the first coming of Christ into our world as Lord, Savior, and God in the flesh. We prepare with decorations, retreats, reflection, anticipation, seasonal music, celebrations, presents, and friendly gatherings. Then Christmas day is over but the church season of Christmastide continues to Epiphany.

Lent takes on a new flavor of detachment, reflection, and mourning over the coming ridicule and suffering of Jesus. We follow his path with anticipation of our sins nailed to the cross, his victory over death, and the assurance of forgiveness and eternal life. At last, Easter! Resurrection celebrations! Christ is risen! He is risen indeed! And Eastertide continues for fifty days, leading us into Pentecost with the coming of the Holy Spirit into each and every heart who place their faith in the Resurrection of our living God, Jesus. With Pentecost, we continue the grand arc of God's saving action in Jesus Christ.

Then we begin the longest season of the church year: Ordinary Time. How will we celebrate? Where are the decorations, presents, special music and focus? For some this becomes a time of "letdown" and perhaps an uneventful time of year. But is it? For now is the time to recognize our place in God's story. In Ordinary Time we take the time to reflect, respond, and integrate into our daily lives all that we've learned and experienced through the previous church seasons. Now we can make connections between Jesus' story and our daily walk. *Ordinary* doesn't mean plain and unimportant; it paints a picture of what God calls us to be and do in everyday life.

We take time to listen to the voice of Jesus through his Word, to be obedient to that which he calls us to do and be. We aim to listen well to people through biblical hospitality and love, and we encourage others to be the hands and feet of Jesus, to yearn for deeper love and faith in Jesus, as we travel through a life of joy, challenge, suffering, and uncertainty. We strive to be holy imitators of Christ. We sing praises to our God, celebrate being redeemed children of God, take pleasure in his creation, grieve with those who grieve and rejoice with those who rejoice. Most of all, we know Jesus saves us, walks with us, rejoices over us, and quiets our souls with his love.

In a few months it will be the season of Advent once again, and the cycle will begin anew. But for now, this is Ordinary Time when we rest assured that Jesus is always with us, never to forsake us, but to help us in our lives, whether it is in the daily routine or the exciting delight of holy surprise. Each day we have the opportunity to make the "ordinary" extraordinary by practicing the presence of the living God, Jesus Christ.

"The discovery of God lies in the daily and the ordinary, not in the spectacular and the heroic. If we cannot find God in the routine times of home and shop, then we will not find him at all. Ours is to be a symphonic piety in which all the activities of work and play and family and worship and sleep are the holy habitats of the eternal."
—Dallas Willard

O LOVE THAT WILL NOT LET ME GO
A HYMN BY GEORGE MATHESON (1882)

O Love that will not let me go,
I rest my weary soul in thee;
I give thee back the life I owe,
That in thine
ocean depths its flow
May richer, fuller be.

O Light that foll'west all my way,
I yield my flick'ring torch to thee;
My heart restores its
borrowed ray,
That in thy sunshine's blaze its day
May brighter, fairer be.

O Joy that seekest me through pain,
I cannot close my heart to thee;
I trace the rainbow
through the rain,
And feel the promise is not vain,
That morn shall tearless be.

O Cross that liftest up my head,
I dare not ask to fly from thee;
I lay in dust life's glory dead,
And from the
ground there blossoms red
Life that shall endless be.

REFLECTION QUESTIONS

Have you ever followed the liturgical year? If so, how did you notice that practice forming or shaping you in your rhythms of life? If not, how is God inviting you to consider this invitation?

On a typical day, what are your first conscious thoughts? In what way do they shape your day and your life?

How do you see your immediate sphere of influence and your "ordinary" days as part of the broader mission and redemptive work of God?

In what ways are God's presence, power, and peace active in your heart, even during your "ordinary" days?

SPIRITUAL PRACTICES

What practices help you recall that you are a beloved child of God in your first waking moments of the day? Try this: As you wake, review your day with God. Give him all the moments ahead of you, and rest in his presence during the day.

Seek hospitality and peace with those nearest to you today. In the evening, review where you experienced God and his leading, assurance, and perhaps even rebuke. As the day ends, ask God to bring about his kingdom through demonstrated acts of peace and love.

Write down a repetitive daily task in your life. As you perform that task, prayerfully ask God to show you the way it shapes you. Journal about it or discuss it with a friend.

A Prayer of Illumination:
We love and celebrate you, Lord Jesus. Thank you for pouring out your Holy Spirit and all his gifts for the journey on which you are sending us. Help us to be aware of your loving presence in all of your creation and all of our life situations. May we joyfully experience your daily presence and leadership. And for all of this, Holy God, we give you thanks and praise! Amen.

ACKNOWLEDGMENTS

No book is ever written by one individual – it takes a team. This is especially true for *Silencio*.

To the 22 writers of the 64 chapters contained herein – thank you, your work is outstanding and you wrote with passion and love for God, his Word, his Church, and his Kingdom. Great will be your reward, dear friends and colleagues in Christ.

To the entire LTI ministry team and board of directors – your role in our shared ministry of formation, discernment, and renewal among leaders and teams is unparalleled and will reap eternal fruit for God's glory.

To the production team – hearty thanks to our project manager Bobby Ryu, proofreader extraordinaire Linda Doll, cover designer Michelle Blackstone, and interior layout expert Priya Paulraj.

All of us on the Leadership Transformations team give glory to God and offer this resource with prayerful hope that it will be used to strengthen, deepen, widen, and expand the hearts of all who partake of the reflective practices offered in *Silencio*. May the ripple effects of our hearts inclined more intimately to Christ be felt for generations to come.

With heartfelt joy in Christ,
Stephen A. Macchia, *Silencio* Editor

SUGGESTED SPIRITUAL FORMATION RESOURCES

—◈—

Looking for additional reading on the spiritual formation topics we've covered in *Silencio*? The Leadership Transformations Team has vetted the following materials and hope they will be a great aid for deepening the vitality of your soul. Many more suggested resources are available in our online store, SpiritualFormationStore.com, and on our website, LeadershipTransformations.org – both of which are continuously updated as new books and online materials are created by the LTI team and our friends and colleagues serving alongside us across the nation and beyond.

PRACTICES

1. LECTIO DIVINA
Contemplative Bible Reading by Richard Peace
Shaped by the Word: The Power of Sacred Scripture in Spiritual Formation by Robert Mulholland

2. LISTENING PRAYER
Armchair Mystic: Easing into Contemplative Prayer by Mark Thibodeaux
Beginning to Pray by Anthony Bloom
When the Soul Listens: Finding Rest and Direction in Contemplative Prayer by Jan Johnson

3. REFLECTION

Journaling by Adam Feldman
Sacred Pathways by Gary Thomas

4. JOURNALING

SoulShaping by Douglas J. Rumford
Spiritual Journaling by Richard Peace
Spiritual Disciplines Handbook by Adele Ahlberg Calhoun

5. EXAMEN

The Examen Prayer: Ignatian Wisdom for Our Lives Today by Timothy M. Gallagher
The Jesuit Guide To (Almost) Everything by James Martin, SJ
Noticing God by Richard Peace

6. CONFESSION

Life Together by Dietrich Bonhoeffer
The Ragamuffin Gospel: Good News for the Bedraggled, Beat-Up, and Burnt Out by Brennan Manning

7. FASTING

A Hunger for God by John Piper
Fasting: Spiritual Freedom Beyond Our Appetites by Lynne M. Baab
Fasting for Spiritual Breakthrough by Elmer L. Towns

8. HOLY EATING

Liturgy of the Ordinary: Sacred Practices in Everyday Life by Tish Harrison Warren
Nourishing Traditions by Sally Fallon

9. SABBATH

The Rest of God: Restoring Your Soul by Restoring Sabbath by Mark Buchanan
Keeping the Sabbath Wholly: Ceasing, Resting, Embracing, Feasting by Marva Dawn
Catch Your Breath: God's Invitation to Sabbath Rest by Don Postema

10. REST

24/6 A Prescription for a Happier Healthier Life by Matthew Sleeth
Sabbath as Resistance: Saying No to the Culture of Now by Walter Brueggemann
Invitations from God by Adele Ahlberg Calhoun

11. GRATITUDE

One Thousand Gifts by Ann Voskamp
The Return of the Prodigal Son by Henri Nouwen

12. RULE OF LIFE

A Spirituality for the 21st Century: The Rule of Benedict by Joan Chittister
Crafting a Rule of Life by Steve Macchia
Rule of Life website, www.ruleoflife.com

13. REORDERING LOVES

Confessions by Augustine
Religious Affections by Jonathan Edwards
Reordered Love, Reordered Lives by David Naugle

14. PERSONAL RETREAT

Learning to Hear God: A Personal Retreat Guide by Jan Johnson
Time Away: A Guide to Personal Retreat by Ben Campbell Johnson, Paul H.Lang
Ready-to-Use Downloadable Personal Retreat Guides produced by Leadership Transformations (www.leadershiptransformations.org/ltistore/Retreat-Guides)

15. PRAYING THE PSALMS

Spirituality of the Psalms by Walter Brueggeman
"Praying the Psalms" in *Soul Keeping* by Howard Baker
Psalms: Prayers of the Heart by Eugene Peterson

POSTURES

16. SILENCE AND SOLITUDE

The Way of the Heart by Henri J.M. Nouwen
Invitation to Solitude and Silence by Ruth Haley Barton

17. HUMILITY

Leadership Transformations' Retreat Guide: Lent (available at SpiritualFormationStore. com).
The Valley of Vision: A Collection of Puritan Prayers and Devotions, ed. by Arthur Bennett

18. DETACHMENT

The Solace of Fierce Landscapes: Exploring Desert and Mountain Spirituality by Belden Lane
Toward Holy Ground: Spiritual Directions for the Second Half of Life by Margaret Guenther

19. ATTENTIVENESS

Practicing the Presence of God by Brother Lawrence
Noticing God by Richard Peace
The Attentive Life: Discerning God's Presence in All Things by Leighton Ford

20. SIMPLICITY
Celebration of Discipline: The Path to Spiritual Growth by Richard J. Foster
Freedom of Simplicity by Richard J. Foster
Simplicity: The Freedom of Letting Go by Richard Rohr

21. DYING TO LIVE
Holy Living and Dying by Jeremy Taylor
The Saints' Everlasting Rest by Richard Baxter

22. WATCHING AND WAITING
The Pursuit of God: The Human Thirst for the Divine by A.W. Tozer
When God Shows Up: How to Recognize the Unexpected Appearances of God in Your Life by R.T. Kendall
With: Reimagining the Way You Relate to God by Skye Jethani

23. HOLY RESTRAINT
The Sayings of the Desert Fathers by Benedicta Ward
The Way of the Heart by Henri Nouwen

24. SELF-KNOWLEDGE
Spiritual Disciplines Handbook, "Confession and Self-Examination" by Adele Calhoun
The Shattered Lantern by Ronald Rolheiser

25. CONTENTMENT
The Rare Jewel of Christian Contentment by Jeremiah Burroughs
The Art of Divine Contentment by Thomas Watson

26. EMBRACING MYSTERY
Doubt, Faith, and Certainty by Anthony Thiselton
The Mystery of God: Theology for Knowing the Unknowable by Christopher Hall and Steven Boyer

27. SEASONS OF THE SOUL
Seasons of the Soul by Bruce Demarest
Spiritual Rhythm by Mark Buchanan

COMPANIONSHIP

28. SPIRITUAL FRIENDSHIP
Spiritual Friendship by Aelred of Rievaulx
Sacred Companions: The Gift of Spiritual Friendship and Direction by David G. Benner

29. SPIRITUAL DIRECTION

Spiritual Direction: A Guide to Giving and Receiving Direction by Gordon T. Smith
The Practice of Spiritual Direction by William A. Barry and William J. Connolly
Spiritual Direction and the Care of Souls: A Guide to Christian Approaches and Practices edited by Gary Moon and David Benner

30. HOSPITALITY

Radical Hospitality by Lonni Collins Pratt
Bread and Wine by Shauna Niequist

31. COMMUNITY

Life Together by Dietrich Bonhoeffer
True Community: The Biblical Practice of Koinonia by Jerry Bridges

32. COMPASSION

Loaves and Fishes by Dorothy Day
Always Enough: God's Miraculous Provision among the Poorest Children on Earth by Rolland and Heidi Baker
Do Justice: A Social Justice Road Map by Kirstin Vander Giessen-Reitsma
Left to Tell: Discovering God Amidst the Rwandan Holocaust by Immaculee Ilibagiza

33. LISTENING TO GOD'S WORD

A Testament of Devotion by Thomas R. Kelly
Sacred Reading: The Ancient Art of Lectio Divina by Michael Casey

34. WITHHOLDING JUDGMENT

The Prodigal God by Tim Keller
The Return of the Prodigal Son by Henri Nouwen
Humility by Andrew Murray

35. BROKEN AND WHOLE

Broken and Whole: A Leader's Path to Spiritual Transformation by Stephen Macchia
Life of the Beloved by Henri Nouwen

36. CONFLICT

Conflict and a Christian Life by Sam Portaro
Renewing Your Church through Healthy Small Groups by Diana Curren Bennett
Joining Together: Group Theory and Group Skills by David W. Johnson and Frank P. Johnson

37. FORGIVENESS
The Hiding Place by Corrie Ten Boom
Forgive and Forget by Lewis Smedes
The Peace Maker by Ken Sande
Caring Enough to Forgive by David Augsburger

CREATIVITY

38. CREATIVITY
Creativity and Divine Surprise by Karla M. Kincannon
A Play-Full Life by Jaco J. Hamman

39. CREATION
The Creator: Living Well in God's World by James Houston
Genesis: A Commentary by Bruce Waltke with Cathi Fredericks

40. CONTEMPLATIVE ARTISTIC EXPRESSION
Coloring the Psalms and Coloring Our Gratitude by Adele Calhoun
"Contemplative Artistic Expressions" TouchPoint by Stephen A. Macchia,
www.LeadershipTransformations.org/ltistore/Reflective-Readings

41. SPACIOUSNESS
Selah, Certificate Program in Spiritual Direction – Leadership Transformations.org
Formed for the Glory of God by Kyle Strobel
Renovation of the Heart by Dallas Willard

42. DISCIPLINE OF PLAY
A Play-Full Life: Slowing Down and Seeking Peace by Jaco J. Hamman
Play: How it Shapes the Brain, Opens the Imagination, and Invigorates the Soul by
Stuart Brown

43. SELF-CARE
The Practice of the Presence of God by Brother Lawrence
Strengthening the Soul of Your Leadership by Ruth Haley Barton
Trauma Stewardship: An Everyday Guide to Caring for Self While Caring for Others
by Laura van Dernoot Lipsky with Connie Burk

44. CELEBRATION
Celebration of Discipline by Richard Foster
The Cross & the Prodigal: Luke 15 Through the Eyes of Middle Eastern Peasants by
Kenneth Bailey

45. ART AND SOUL
The Creative Call: An Artist's Response to the Way of the Spirit by Janice Elsheimer
Walking on Water: Reflections on Art and Faith by Madeleine L'Engle
www.internationalartsmovement.org | www.civa.org (Christians in Visual Arts)

46. BODY AND SOUL
Care of Mind, Care of Spirit by Gerald May
Anatomy of the Soul by Curt Thompson

SERVICE

47. REFORMATION OF THE SOUL
A Guide to Prayer for All Who Walk With God by Rueben P. Job
With: Reimagining the Way you Relate to God by Skye Jethani
The Prodigal God by Tim Keller

48. VOCATION
God at Work: Your Christian Vocation in All of Life by Gene Edward Veith, Jr.
Rising to the Call: Discover the Ultimate Purpose of Your Life by Os Guinness

49. PERSECUTION
Pray for the World: A New Prayer Resource from Operation World by Patrick Johnstone
I Am N: Inspiring Stories of Christians Facing Islamic Extremists by The Voice of the Martyrs
Voice of the Martyrs website: www.persecution.com

50. RECEPTIVITY
Emotionally Healthy Spirituality by Pete Scazzero
Shaped by the Word by M. Robert Mullholland, Jr.

51. GENEROSITY
Journey of Generosity, GenerousGiving.org
Celebration of Discipline by Richard J. Foster
I Like Giving by Brad Formsma
One Hen by Katie Smith Milway (children's book)

52. A LIFE OF WORSHIP
Sacred Pathways: Discover Your Soul's Path to God by Gary L. Thomas
Abide in Christ by Andrew Murray
Surrender to Love by David Benner

SEASONS

53. THE CHURCH YEAR
Book of Common Prayer, the Collects for the Church Year
Living the Christian Year: Time to Inhabit the Story of God by Bobby Gross
Receiving the Day: Christian Practices for Opening the Gift of Time by Dorothy Bass

54. ADVENT LONGING
Watch for the Light: Readings for Advent and Christmas by Plough Publishing House
Advent at Ephesus, Benedictines of Mary, Decca Records (cd recording)
Evensong by Gail Godwin

55. A CHILD-LIKE ADVENT
Young Children and Worship by Sonja M. Stewart and Jerome W. Berryman
Best Practices in Children's Faith Formation by John Roberto and Katie Pfiffner
The Promise of Christmas by Steve Macchia

56. INCARNATION
God Is in the Manger: Reflections on Advent and Christmas by Dietrich Bonhoeffer
The Greatest Gift by Ann Voskamp

57. CHRISTMAS PRESENCE
Preparing for Jesus by Walter Wangerin
The Greatest Gift and *Unwrapping the Greatest Gift* by Ann Voskamp
Let Every Heart Prepare Him Room by Ted Wueste

58. EPIPHANY
Light upon Light: A Literary Guide to Prayer for Advent, Christmas, and Epiphany,
compiled by Sarah Arthur
Pray for the World: A New Prayer Resource from Operation World, Patrick Johnstone,
Jason Mandryk, Molly Wall

59. LENT: A SEASON OF PREPARATION
Listen: Praying in a Noisy World by Rueben P. Job
Reliving the Passion by Walter Wangerin Jr.
A Season for the Spirit by Martin L. Smith, SSJE

60. LENT: A TRAIL OF TEARS
Outstretched Arms of Grace: A 40-Day Lenten Devotional by Stephen A. Macchia and
Journal with Discussion Questions by Ted Wueste and Terry Montague
Journey to the Cross: Devotions for Lent by Will Walker and Kendal Haug
Make Room: A Child's Guide to Lent and Easter by Laura Alary

61. EASTER RESURRECTION
The Christ of the Empty Tomb by James Montgomery Boice
Jesus: A Gospel by Henri Nouwen

62. ASCENSION
Calvin's Ladder: A Spiritual Theology of Ascent and Ascension by Julie Canlis
Ascension and Ecclesia by Douglas Farrow

63. PENTECOST: WAITING ATTENTIVELY
A Quiet Pentecost: Inviting the Spirit into Congregational Life by Dwight H. Judy
The Broken Way by Ann Voskamp
Life of the Beloved by Henri Nouwen

64. ORDINARY TIME
Living the Christian Year by Bobby Gross
Liturgy of the Ordinary by Tish Harrison Warren

All suggested Spiritual Formation Resources can be found on LTI's online store:
www.SpiritualFormationStore.com

About

LEADERSHIP
TRANSFORMATIONS INC.
FORMATION | DISCERNMENT | RENEWAL

VISION, MISSION AND MINISTRY OVERVIEW

Leadership Transformations, Inc. is a nonprofit organization founded in 2003. From its inception, LTI has been an important part of the national spiritual formation movement serving in a variety of ways, teaching, coaching and guiding leaders into a deeper, more intimate walk with Christ. *We believe as the leader goes, so goes the organization, and as the soul of the leader goes, so goes the leader.* Therefore, out of the depth of a leader's soul comes vitality in their service to others. Spiritual leadership development is and will remain our top priority.

OUR VISION

For Christian congregations and organizations to be filled with leaders who place spiritual formation, discernment and renewal above all other leadership priorities.

OUR MISSION

To cultivate vibrant spirituality and attentive discernment among Christian leaders and teams. To accomplish this mission, the staff, volunteers and board members, together with strategic partners, LTI will work to create formal and informal opportunities for leaders and teams to:

- Embrace a lifestyle of Sabbath rest and renewal.
- Experience spiritual reflection, biblical truth and attentive discernment.

- Acknowledge the Holy Spirit's constant presence and work in their lives.
- Attend to new insights with open-handed receptivity and initiative.
- Sense a renewed invitation to discover God's call on their lives and ministries.

OUR MINISTRIES

Emmaus: Spiritual Leadership Communities
Selah: Certificate Program in Spiritual Direction
Soul Care Retreats and Soul Sabbaths
Spiritual Formation Groups
Spiritual Health Assessments
Spiritual Discernment for Teams
Sabbatical Planning
Spiritual Formation Resources *www.spiritualformationstore.com*
Pierce Center for Disciple-Building *Partnership with Gordon-Conwell Seminary*

Resources

OF

LEADERSHIP
TRANSFORMATIONS ᴵⁿᶜ.

---

www.LeadershipTransformations.org – our home base website for up-to-the minute information on the ministry of Leadership Transformations – our programs, resources, overview, team, partnerships, blog, newsletters, and calendar of events

www.SpiritualFormationStore.com – hundreds of LTI-created and vetted materials classified in 25 different categories available for spiritual formation enthusiasts and practitioners

www.HealthyChurch.net – LTI's unique web-based "Church Health Assessment Tool" (also known as CHAT) – a listening and assessment tool for congregations and communities worldwide

www.RuleOfLife.com – dedicated website designed for those who are crafting their personal rule of life individually and in community

Made in the USA
Monee, IL
06 December 2019